D0338436

JESSE JACKSON

Recent Titles in Greenwood Biographies

JESSE JACKSON

A Biography

Roger Bruns

GREENWOOD BIOGRAPHIES

GREENWOOD RRESS
WESTPORT, CONNECTICUT • LONDON

Library of Congress Cataloging-in-Publication Data

Bruns, Roger.
  Jesse Jackson: a biography / by Roger Bruns
    p.cm. — (Greenwood biographies, ISSN 1540-4900)
  Includes bibliographical references and index
  ISBN 0–313–33138–3 (alk. paper)
  1. Jackson, Jesse, 1941- 2. African Americans—Biography. 3. Civil rights work-
ers—United States—Biography. 4. Presidential candidates—United States—Biography.
I. Title II. Series.
E185.97.J25B78 2005
973.927'092—dc22   2004026939

British Library Cataloguing-in-Publication Data is available.

Copyright © 2005 by Roger Bruns

All rights reserved. No portion of this book may be
reproduced, by any process or technique, without the
express written consent of the publisher.

Library of Congress Catalog Card Number: 2004026939
ISBN: 0–313–33138–3
ISSN: 1540–4900

First published in 2005

Greenwood Press, 88 Post Road West, Westport, CT 06881
An imprint of Greenwood Publishing Group, Inc.
www.greenwood.com

Printed in the United States of America

The paper used in this book complies with the
Permanent Paper Standard issued by the National
Information Standards Organization (Z39.48–1984).

10 9 8 7 6 5 4 3 2 1

CONTENTS

CONTENTS

Photo essay follows page 58

SERIES FOREWORD

In response to high school and public library needs, Greenwood developed this distinguished series of full-length biographies specifically for student use. Prepared by field experts and professionals, these engaging biographies are tailored for high school students who need challenging yet accessible biographies. Ideal for secondary school assignments, the length, format, and subject areas are designed to meet educators' requirements and students' interests.

Greenwood offers an extensive selection of biographies spanning all curriculum-related subject areas, including social studies, the sciences, literature and the arts, history, and politics, as well as popular culture, covering public figures and famous personalities from all time periods and backgrounds, both historic and contemporary, who have made an impact on American and/or world culture. Greenwood biographies were chosen on the basis of comprehensive feedback from librarians and educators. Consideration was given to both curriculum relevance and inherent interest. The result is an intriguing mix of the well known and the unexpected, the saints and sinners from long-ago history and contemporary pop culture. Readers will find a wide array of subject choices from fascinating crime figures like Al Capone to inspiring pioneers like Margaret Mead, from the greatest minds of our time like Stephen Hawking to the most amazing success stories of our day like J. K. Rowling.

While the emphasis is on fact, not glorification, the books are meant to be fun to read. Each volume provides in-depth information about the subject's life from birth through childhood, the teen years, and adulthood.

A thorough account relates family background and education, traces personal and professional influences, and explores struggles, accomplishments, and contributions. A timeline highlights the most significant life events against a historical perspective. Bibliographies supplement the reference value of each volume.

INTRODUCTION

He was an unlikely prospect for fame. What was the chance that he might become somebody of influence, somebody of international renown? The odds were infinitesimal.

Born in 1941 to an unwed, 16-year-old mother in a poor, segregated section of Greenville, South Carolina, he learned quickly what he could not do. He could not ride in the front seating area of buses. He could not enter the major department stores downtown, go to movie theaters, drink out of public water fountains unless they were labeled "colored," eat at downtown lunch counters, attend a public school near his house that was reserved for white children, swim in public swimming pools, use the downtown public library, walk on the courthouse lawn, live outside a pre-scribed area of town, or even use public restrooms. He could not do these things because he was black.

But the young boy had certain qualities that transcended his station—intelligence, drive, and a stubbornness to fight back and succeed. Jesse Jackson knew, even then, that he was somebody.

Since his days as a student at North Carolina Agricultural & Techni-cal State University (North Carolina A&T), Jackson was a follower and associate of civil rights leader, Martin Luther King Jr. Following King's assassination in 1968, Jackson emerged as the country's most dynamic leader for racial justice and the economic empowerment of minority citi-zens. He came to national prominence at a wrenching time in the nation's history, with racial polarization and hatred spilling onto the streets, with thousands of American soldiers losing their lives in the battlefields of Vietnam and contentious political acrimony at home over the war and its consequences.

A powerful orator and indefatigable organizer, Jackson established himself as one of the most dynamic forces for social and political action in both the national and the international arenas, campaigning for human rights and social justice. Through such social action projects as Operation Breadbasket, Operation PUSH, and the National Rainbow Coalition, as well as his own candidacy for the Democratic nomination for president in 1984 and 1988, Jackson became a worldwide spokesman for the minorities, the marginalized, and the poor. He and his campaigns have attracted fame and admiration; they have also generated hostility and scorn from his opponents.

For his work on behalf of racial and social justice, Jackson has been awarded at least 40 honorary degrees, and for over a decade he has been listed among the Gallup Poll's 10 most admired men.

His runs for the presidency mobilized millions of voters and encouraged thousands of individuals across the country to vote for the first time. His candidacy voiced vital social and racial issues on the national level and, for the first time, raised the real possibility that a black could win the nation's highest office. Jackson's two presidential campaigns broke new ground in U.S. politics. In 1984, he ran a strong third in the Democratic primaries, amassing over 3 million votes. His Democratic convention speech, a call to "Keep Hope Alive," electrified the crowd and millions of viewers on television. In 1988, he won several major primaries and more than doubled his votes from his 1984 candidacy.

Since the 1970s, he has conducted a number of sensational diplomatic overtures, several of which were independently organized and not aligned to the presidential administration in Washington. In 1984, Jackson secured the release of a captured Navy pilot, Lieutenant Robert Goodman, from Syria and the release of 48 Cuban and Cuban American prisoners in Cuba. In 1991, his diplomatic efforts resulted in the release of hundreds of hostages being held by Iraqi President Saddam Hussein. He helped negotiate the release of American hostages in Kuwait and Iraq in 1990 and the release of U.S. soldiers held hostage in Kosovo in 1999.

He has visited thousands of high schools, academic institutions, and prisons, challenging young people to secure an education and to stay drug free, and has set up several national programs to promote those goals.

In 1991, the U.S. Post Office put his likeness on a pictorial postal cancellation. This was only the second time in history that a living person received such an honor. On August 9, 2000, President Bill Clinton awarded Jackson the Presidential Medal of Freedom, the nation's highest civilian honor given for meritorious service to the United States.

Along with the accomplishments, however, Jackson has, from his earliest days, sparked towering animosity. Some of it results from his hard-charging nature, his liberal ideology, and his aggressiveness to push himself front and center. It is also from a pool of resentment and bitterness built up among his enemies, those whose interests Jackson has attacked, those threatened by political and social activities, and those who regard him personally as less than honest. Even among political allies, he has provoked hostility for invading what they regarded as personal turf and for what they consider reckless self-promotion.

His economic boycotts and threats of boycotts against such corporations as Coca-Cola and Texaco have been criticized by some businessmen as extortion and shakedowns. Others have insinuated that his management of several organizations was nothing short of corrupt, although a number of investigations have not proven those allegations. He has been attacked for negotiating with so-called terrorist and communist organizations, such as Fidel Castro and the Palestine Liberation Organization. He has been accused of nestling too closely with radical black extremist groups. He has had to fight off charges that he was anti-Semitic, especially after a notorious remark during the 1984 presidential campaign referring to New York City as "Hymietown," an outburst for which he has repeatedly apologized. In 2003, Jackson admitted that he fathered a child out of wedlock.

The same overpowering ambition that has led to his successes, many observers have noted, is also the source of his failings. A tireless advocate and organizer, he also never misses an opportunity for self-promotion. Infused with a deep sense of mission and purpose, he also moves from project to project and crisis to crisis in bursts of productivity, sometimes without a successful resolution.

Jackson has carved a truly unique role in his life. Although an ordained minister, he has never been the minister of a church and has never written or spoken extensively about the gospel or sectarian issues. His theological role is entirely infused with his campaigns for social action and change. It is the juggling of his roles in the spiritual and political spheres that has been his greatest challenge.

Jesse Jackson is an extraordinary man of action and contradiction, a traveler of quixotic roads. This is the story of his journey.

TIMELINE OF EVENTS IN THE LIFE OF JESSE JACKSON

8 October, 1941	Jesse Louis Burns (Jesse Jackson) born.
1956	Takes his stepfather's name. Becomes Jesse Louis Jackson.
Spring 1959	Graduates from Sterling High School in Greenville, South Carolina.
Fall 1959–Spring 1960	Attends University of Illinois.
Fall 1961	Transfers to North Carolina A&T.
31 December 1962	Marries Jacqueline Lavinia Brown.
April/May/June 1963	Becomes a leader of civil rights demonstrations in Greensboro, North Carolina.
6 June 1963	Arrested in Greensboro for "inciting to riot and disturbing the peace and dignity of the state."
May 1964	Graduates from North Carolina A&T.
September 1964	Enters the Chicago Theological Seminary.
March 1965	After watching attacks on civil rights marchers on television, Jackson is among thousands who head to Selma, Alabama, for protest. Meets civil rights leader Dr. Martin Luther King Jr.; asks him for a job.
Spring 1966	Becomes head of Chicago chapter of Southern Christian Leadership Conference's (SCLC) Operation Breadbasket, a movement promoting better employment for blacks through peaceful boycotts and negotiations. Launches first economic boycott.

Summer 1966	Among the leaders of King's protest marches supporting the right of blacks to live in formerly all-white neighborhoods in Chicago.
Summer 1967	Becomes the national director of Operation Breadbasket.
4 April 1968	King assassinated in Memphis, Tennessee, while there to support striking garbage workers; Jackson, at motel during assassination, appears on television with King's blood on his shirt.
30 June 1968	Jackson becomes an ordained minister at Chicago's Fellowship Missionary Baptist Church.
December 1971	Resigns from SCLC and starts Operation PUSH (People United to Serve Humanity).
Summer 1972	Jackson and William Singer unseat Chicago Mayor Richard Daley delegate slate at the Democratic convention in Miami.
1977	Founds PUSH/Excel, a program to encourage inner-city kids in their schoolwork.
1979	In a controversial visit to Middle East, meets with Palestinian leader Yasser Arafat.
October 1983	Enters the 1984 Democratic presidential race.
December 1983	In Syria, frees downed U.S. pilot Robert Goodman.
February 1984	Labels New York City "Hymietown" in comments reported by the press; he apologizes.
1984	Founds the National Rainbow Coalition, a political action organization dedicated to bringing together the various minority populations.
March 1988	With his victory in Michigan, Jackson takes the lead in popular votes and delegates in the 1988 Democratic presidential primary. Eventually loses to Massachusetts Governor Michael Dukakis.
1989	Moves to Washington, D.C., and wins election as the district's "Shadow Senator," a largely ceremonial, nonvoting member of Congress.
September 1991	Wins the release of hundreds of foreign nationals being held in Kuwait by Iraqi leader Saddam Hussein.
Fall 1991	Announces he will not run for president in 1992.
1996	Returns to Operation PUSH in Chicago.

February 1997	Proposes an initiative to help close the learning gap between black and white children in part by emphasizing the role of parents.
October 1997	Becomes President Clinton's "Special Envoy for the President and Secretary of State for the Promotion of Democracy in Africa."
January 1998	Launches "The Wall Street Project" to encourage greater black participation in American capitalism.
November 1998	Leads a four-nation tour of West Africa, including stops in Nigeria, Guinea, Sierra Leone, and Ghana.
29 April 1999	During the Kosovo war, leaves for Belgrade, Serbia, to negotiate with Serb leader Slobodan Milosevic for the release of three U.S. prisoners of war captured on the Macedonian border while patrolling with a UN peacekeeping unit.
August 2000	Receives Presidential Medal of Freedom from President Bill Clinton.
January 2001	Admits fathering daughter out of wedlock.
February 2003	Speaks at massive protest in London against war in Iraq.
31 March 2004	Signs contract with Clear Channel Radio as talk show host.
Spring 2004	Leads voter registration drives and other political action events against administration of President George W. Bush.

Chapter 1

"OUR TIME HAS COME"

On Tuesday evening, July 17, 1984, from the hall of the Democratic National Convention in San Francisco's George Mascone Center, CBS television anchor Dan Rather told millions of viewers, "We don't often say this, but it's time to get the children in, time to get the grandmother in. The anticipation here, at least in this hall, is that Jesse Jackson's address—whatever you think of him, rightly or wrongly, whether you like him or not like him—may be one for the history books."[1]

Reverend Jesse Jackson had come to the convention as the first black American presidential candidate in history to mount a serious run for the presidency. He was the first ever to win a presidential election primary race and the first to receive Electoral College votes, amassing almost 400 delegates behind the winner, Walter Mondale, and second-place finisher Gary Hart. Through the primaries, more than 3.2 million Americans voted for Jackson. He had come to the convention with a status never before achieved by a black politician. He came hoping to play a prominent role at the convention in shaping the party platform toward emphasis on social justice. He also was there, he said, to help heal the divisions within the Democratic Party at a time when President Ronald Reagan, primed to win a second term, had led the Republican Party to an ascendancy of political power in the country.

Although Jackson realized that the dream of a black candidate actually winning the presidency would not be realized in 1984, he also knew that he had made a remarkable run, mobilizing an unprecedented grassroots organization and energizing minority voters, many of who cast their first vote in the 1984 primaries. His "Rainbow Coalition" of supporters, including blacks, Native Americans, Hispanics, Asian Americans, Arab Americans, women, and other groups who in the past had exercised little political power, were now, together, a force with which to be reckoned. He had said many times that the American flag was red, white, and blue, but America was a mosaic of red, yellow, brown, black, and white hues, people from many backgrounds and cultures and all with hopes and aspirations for themselves and their children. With this speech, the 43-year-old civil rights activist and organizer had assumed a mantle of leadership for huge numbers of American citizens who felt ignored in the political process and left behind in a land of plenty.

Across the country, many of them jostled for a place in front of television sets to hear the oratory from the renowned speaker. Some had heard him on the political stump or before crowds of teenagers as he exhorted them to back away from the temptations of life in the backstreets and on the run and to find within themselves the courage, energy, and dedication to make a difference, to allow themselves to dream, to realize that all could fit in and have a place. Others were going to hear Jackson's message for the first time.

As in most of his major addresses, the beginning of the speech was modulated in pacing and contemplative in substance. Jackson gripped the podium with both hands, stared over the vast assemblage, and began speaking at 11 P.M. Throughout the address, the television audience, according to later surveys, continued to increase, reaching 33 million viewers.

He quickly vowed to support the nominee of the Democratic Party, Walter Mondale, and expressed wholehearted backing of Mondale's decision to add to the ticket as vice-presidential candidate Geraldine Ferraro, a member of the U.S. House of Representatives from New York State. She would be the first woman ever to be vice-presidential candidate on a major party ticket.

Jackson apologized for his insensitive remark during the campaign regarding the Jewish people and assured the audience that his words that day were not spoken from the heart. "I am not a perfect servant," he said, "I am a public servant. As I develop and serve, be patient. God is not finished with me yet." He talked about how Christians and Jews were too bound by their shared Judeo-Christian heritage and have suffered too much for too long from racism, sexism, and militarism to be divided one from another. They must "share hands" and keep common ground for the common purpose.[2]

As he began a recitation of grievances against the Republican Party and President Reagan, Jackson's words began with increasing intensity and volume to fill the hall. What the party in power had done in the first four years of the administration, he charged, was a moral outrage, enriching the pockets of the big business and wealthy Americans at the expense of the vast numbers of poor and middle class. He lamented the infant mortality rate in some American cities that equaled that of Third World countries; attacked cuts in education and the abandonment of environmental concerns to the whims of developers; charged that the war policies of the administration, especially in Latin America, had made a dangerous world even more dangerous and had lined the pockets of military contractors; and lambasted the failure of the administration in alleviating poverty. Instead, he said, for those Americans without jobs, without the chance to get an education or the ability to pay for health costs, the Reagan administration had committed against them nothing less than a crime that must be redressed.

The scene in San Francisco late that evening had no precedent. Here was a black American, a preacher, social reformer, and politician, electrifying an audience inside that was still overwhelmingly white, giving them common cause with those in their party who were not white and not wealthy.

He called for nothing less than a rebuilding of America's priorities—help for those who need it, from the poor to the elderly to the physically disabled; justice and equal treatment for all in American society regardless of their station in life; a negotiated reduction in nuclear arms that menace the entire world; an emphasis on education and for encouraging and supporting committed teachers; programs to ensure health care for all and decent housing; a concentrated effort to provide adequate jobs for the unemployed; and a leadership in Washington that levels with the American people and represents the interests of all and not just those with power and money. This must not be a government that measures greatness by its concentrated wealth or military power. "Jesus said that we should not be judged by the bark we wear but by the fruit that we bear. Jesus said that we must measure greatness by how we treat the least of these."

This was more of a sermon now, filled with biblical allusions, the rolling gospel cadences reaching a rhythmic beat. Roars of approval swelled over the crowd, the hall now seeming more like a revival tent than a political convention. The sound was now like that from reformers and preachers in the early days of the civil rights marches, the sounds of the black churches whose messages rocked with crescendos of purpose. Jackson, who in the 1960s led demonstrations against libraries and lunch counters in the South, held mesmerizing oratorical power for nearly an hour. He concluded,

> Our time has come. Our time has come. Suffering breeds character. Character breeds faith. In the end, faith will not disappoint. Our time has come. Our faith, hope, and dreams will prevail. Our time has come. Weeping has endured for nights, but now joy cometh in the morning. Our time has come. No grave can hold our body down. Our time has come. No lie can live forever. Our time has come. We must leave racial battleground and come to economic common ground and moral higher ground. America, our time has come. We come from disgrace to amazing grace. Our time has come. Give me your tired, give me your poor, your huddled masses who yearn to breathe free and come November, there will be a change because our time has come.

Many called the speech one of the best they had ever heard. Walter Mondale himself said it was "one of the great speeches of our time."[3]

One woman remembered years later her family gathering around the television that night to hear Jackson. "I felt something very important was happening," she said. "My mother, who hadn't shed tears in public since my father's funeral, was crying and whispering 'Amen.' When Jackson finished speaking, I stood on our back porch and took in the sounds of stomping feet, cheers and clapping coming from our neighbors' homes. This was our moment and it was golden."[4]

NOTES

1. *New York Times*, July 18, 1984.

2. All quotations from this speech are from "Jesse Jackson: 1984 Democratic National Convention Address, http://www.americanrhetoric.com/speeches/jessejackson1984dnc.htm.

3. *New York Times*, July 18, 1984.

4. Kimberley Jane Wilson, "Shakedown: A Shocking Jesse Jackson Biography," http://www.nationalcenter.org/P21NVWilsonJackson602.html.

Chapter 2

SOUTH CAROLINA

Jesse Jackson was nearly born in secret. There was little celebration and a strong sense of shame at 20 Haynie Street in Greenville, South Carolina, when he entered the world on October 8, 1941. His mother, Helen Burns, was an unmarried 17-year-old high school student; his father was a married man who lived next door and already a stepfather of three. His father's name was Noah Robinson. He was a tall, muscular, former boxer who now worked in a local textile mill, grading the quality of cotton. Almost twice the age of Helen Burns, he was an admired member of the community.

A beautiful and talented girl who planned to pursue a singing career, Helen had been nearly shunned by the community when she first admitted her pregnancy. One of her friends later remarked that Helen had it all—looks, that fantastic voice, and a vivacious personality. She was star quality at Sterling High School, and she could confidently expect a number of colleges to offer music scholarships. Beyond college, some of her friends said, might be the concert stage for this gifted young woman or a popular singing career. She had become the lead majorette at the high school and had performed in dance shows that toured the area. But now she was about to have a baby at 17 years of age without a husband, without a job, and with most of her family and friends hushed about the birth.

At the Springfield Baptist Church, where Helen's thrilling voice had soared through the wooden rafters on many Sunday mornings, the congregation nearly ostracized the teenager because of the pregnancy. Hurt by the slurs and vicious rumor mongering that swept through the local community,

Helen, for a time, had considered an abortion. After much agonizing and with the advice of her minister, she decided to have the baby.

The physician at Helen's side that chilly October day in the black neighborhood was a white man, a friend of the family for whom Matilda "Tibby" Burns, Helen's mother, worked. Tibby herself knew the experience of having a child in her teenage years. When Helen was born, Tibby was only 13 years old.

It was mostly a sense of relief that filled the room when the 7-pound, 4-ounce boy entered the world. Lest the neighbors would hear, Helen had insisted that everyone be as quiet as possible. No fuss or hallelujahs welcomed the newborn. Although the days ahead would be challenging, both the child and the mother were healthy. Helen named the boy Jesse Louis Burns, after Noah Robinson's father, Jesse Louis Robinson.

It was in this Haynie Street neighborhood, a congested area where most of Greenville's black population lived, amidst its dirt lanes, narrow wooden frame houses with tin roofs, no running water, small front porches, and outhouses in the backyards, that young Jesse spent his first years. Many of the houses were in such condition, with wood covering some of the windows and open holes, that it was difficult to tell whether they were coming down or going up. Others, solid brick houses where the more affluent blacks lived, were intermixed with the dilapidated in a kind of quilt of poverty and middle class because blacks who acquired relative wealth could not move into white neighborhoods.

Like most of the black residents of the neighborhood, Jesse's parentage could be traced not only to African slave roots but also to the Cherokee Indians who once roamed the hills of the Piedmont, hunting game. One of Jesse's great-grandmothers was part Cherokee and also a slave. There was also Irish in his blood, a great-grandfather who once served as sheriff of Greenville County.

Gradually, and mostly with reluctance, the neighbors and church members accepted Helen and her child. With much help from her mother, Tibby, Helen learned to take care of young Jesse through his earliest years. Although Noah Robinson took no responsibility in raising his son, Jesse's grandmother was known to have charged next door on numerous occasions to demand from Robinson an extra bottle of milk or some other groceries for her impoverished daughter and grandson. Years later, Robinson said, "I never denied Jesse. Before he was born I gave him my father's name and my own middle name. I love Jesse."[1]

When Jesse was two years old, his mother married a hardworking, quiet man named Charles Henry Jackson who had a job shining shoes in a downtown barbershop. Charles moved into the Haynie Street home with Helen, Tibby, and young Jesse. Shortly after the marriage, Charles was inducted into the army and left his new wife and family for World War II. Her dreams of college and a singing career now on hold, Helen began to study to become a beautician.

In his early years, Jesse was never told that the imposing man next door was his real father. Instead, Charles Jackson, with his marriage to Helen, assumed that role. Helen would show Jesse pictures of Charles in his army uniform and tell the boy that daddy would return shortly. Eventually, the family gave Jesse the name of Jackson. "I didn't want him to grow up thinking he was different," Charles explained later.[2]

It was not until he was about nine years old that the young boy discovered the truth about his father. Jackson always played down the revelation. "It was no traumatic moment," he would say. "It happened so smoothly it was never a hitch.... I had two men in my life who loved me very much.[3]

But the inner tension that Jesse felt toward the two men—his real father, Noah Robinson, and Charles Jackson—played on the boy's emotions throughout his childhood and teenage years. On the few occasions when Robinson and the boy talked, Jesse seemed almost mesmerized. Robinson told him stories about his boxing days. He talked about the fact that his own father and his father's twin brother were preachers who had often acted as partners in orating from the pulpit, a duo of look-alike and sound-alike soul savers.

When Noah Robinson and his wife became the parents of two additional children and after Robinson's financial situation improved, he moved his family into a much more elaborate, expensive house in the black neighborhood of Fieldcrest Village. The house seemed to Jesse almost mansion-like in its dimensions. It is not surprising that Jesse's jealously toward Robinson's children grew and that he had to fight back deep regrets and hostility toward his own circumstances and toward his mother, stepfather, and others with whom he shared their own small, shack-like house.

Nevertheless, Charles Jackson, looking back on those years of Jesse's childhood, could say, "We were never poor. We never wanted for anything. We've never been on welfare because I was never without a job. We never begged anybody for a dime. And my family never went hungry a day in their lives."[4] Jackson officially adopted Jesse in 1957.

In 1954, when Jesse was 13 years old, Charles Jackson, who had managed to land a job as a custodian at the Post Office building, was able to move his family from Haynie Street to a housing project building. For Jesse and the other family members, the move into a brick building with hot and cold running water, a place where the family did not have to use wallpaper to fill cracks that let in the winter winds, a place with even a doorbell, was glorious.

THE STRANGLE OF SEGREGATION

In Jesse Jackson's youth, black Americans still had a long climb toward equality. Even though several generations had passed since the Civil War, a large segment of the population, because of its color, remained isolated, poor, and with opportunities so limited as to stifle even the most energetic and talented.

For the black community in Greenville, as with black communities across the country, much of American society was off limits. Housing in the better-developed sections of town was off limits. Schools and churches had either white or black congregations. If a black individual went downtown, the restaurants and lunch counters in department stores were off limits, as were theaters and even public libraries. On public conveyances such as buses and trains, blacks were separated from whites, as they were in public courtrooms and other official buildings. Even more dispiriting and degrading were the signs at water fountains and swimming pools and other public places indicating "Whites Only." Blacks had to pay taxes but did not have the right to vote. The lawn of the state capitol was off limits. Whites could take pictures of their children and each other and their dogs on that lawn; blacks could not. From the earliest days of childhood, Jesse, as did other blacks, learned limitations rather than possibilities.

Jackson later remembered he and his friends joking that segregation did not affect them; that they were not really thirsty that day, or hungry, or anxious to see a movie; that they had other things to do and other people to see; and that the whites could go about their own business because Jesse and his friends did not want to have anything to do with them anyway. It was a way to deal with the humiliation, a way to mask the grinding frustration and fear. He recognized, even at a very early age, that the social system was overpowering and unfair. He later talked about the fact that his father performed janitorial duties at several of the white churches in Greenville but could not attend services on Sunday mornings.

Jackson and his friends sometimes walked to Furman University, a private liberal arts school about five miles north of Greenville, to sell soft drinks and peanuts at football games and to watch cars of the spectators for a fee. Helen often did laundry for the college's fraternity members, washing and ironing for 20 cents an item. During the games, the troupe would march up a grassy hill behind the stadium to see as much of the game as they could. Little did they realize that many of the undergraduates had a name for the spot on the hill. They called it "The Crow's Nest."

Years later, when Jackson spoke to groups of young inner-city blacks, he could tell them that he knew firsthand what they were facing. He could tell them that he, too, had faced a future against the odds. "I do understand," he would say. "I was born to a teenage mother, who was born to a teenage mother. How do I understand? I never slept under the same roof with my natural father one night in my life. I understand."[5]

On another occasion, he declared, "I know people saying you're nothing and nobody and can never be anything. I understand when you have no real last name. I understand. Because our very genes cry out for confirmation."[6]

Jesse attended the segregated Nicholtown Elementary School, which was a five-mile walk from his home. Only a few blocks away stood an elementary school for white children.

Bright and attractive, a boy with a seemingly endless well of conversation from which to draw, Jesse also had energy and drive that, from early on, marked him in the eyes of friends, members of the community, and especially teachers. Assertive and demanding attention, he also showed a fierce edge of competitiveness.

From his early years, he was physically imposing, always towering over his fellow classmates. As each year into his adolescence passed and he began to attend Sterling High School, friends and relatives all remarked that he looked more and more like Noah Robinson—tall, good looking, with a jaunty but imperial demeanor. People began to notice his powerful physique.

In addition to his schoolwork and extracurricular activities, Jackson also took numerous jobs to help out the family. He delivered stove wood, caddied at Greenville's country club, waited tables at an airport restaurant, and worked at the Poinsett Hotel.

Spurred on by both his grandmother and mother, Jackson also learned to volunteer in the community. For a time, before he was 10 years old, Jesse read newspapers to illiterate adults, an activity in which his mother had engaged for several years. Unlike many from the neighborhood, Helen had completed her schooling and graduated from Sterling. She was able to read. Many older men and women from the neighborhood who were illiterate would ask Helen to help fill out Social Security papers and help them with other paperwork and even with their simple financial dealings.

They never forgot her kindnesses. On one occasion, when Jessie's family was particularly hurting financially, a gift of six bags of groceries unexpectedly appeared on the family porch. There was no note. The next day, they learned it was from one of the men Helen had assisted. The incident left a special impression on Jesse. "This was a very spiritual experience," Jesse said, "and made an imprint on my mind. The reason there was no writing on the groceries was that Mr. Dave couldn't write. That was really 'bread cast on the water,' returning toasted, with butter on it."[7]

Jesse would always remember that sense of community sharing. It enabled his own family and others to survive their challenging circumstances.

Both his mother and his grandmother emphasized to the boy the importance of education. As Tibby worked as a domestic for Greenville's white upper classes, she would often borrow books from her employers for Jesse to read and bring home magazines they no longer needed. She herself was illiterate. But she had encouraged her daughter to continue her studies in high school, and both she and Helen soon began to recognize Jesse's extraordinary intelligence and curiosity.

Unlike many of his friends from the neighborhood, Jesse had only a few confrontations with the police during his teenage years. He did remember that law enforcement did seem "to get a kick out of breaking down the front door if you didn't answer quickly enough. When I was a little kid, we'd run and hide under the house at the sight of a police car. Later on, they locked us up for things like vagrancy or cursing." A few of his friends never made it past high school, killed either in fights between each other or in skirmishes with the police. Jackson later recalled a police action that became legendary in the neighborhood. One policeman, Jesse said, became infamous for locking up a black man for "reckless eyeballing" a white woman from 100 feet away.[8]

Because of the influence of both his mother and his grandmother, who were regular churchgoers, religious activities had a major influence on Jesse in his early years. Sunday school was a regular event, and when he was in the third grade, Jesse joined the church.

He especially remembered the commanding presence of the minister, Reverend D. S. Sample of the Long Branch Baptist Church. As Jesse listened, transfixed to the pulsating rhythms of the gospel belted out in thunderous beats, with the congregation clapping and vocally urging the preacher on to greater heights, he understood the power not only of oratory but also of the gospel message. This was a pickax religion, a religion from the gut in which faith was mountain moving and in which every member of the congregation, shouting amens and swinging to the spirit, had a part regardless of their everyday circumstances. In the church pews was a democracy before God, and it had nothing to do with black or white, rich or poor. Watching Reverend Sample, Jesse could feel himself up there at the pulpit, leading the spiritual charge.

When he was about nine years old, Jesse gave a speech at a church Christmas pageant. So impressed was the congregation with the precocious young man that they sent him to a national Sunday school convention in Charlotte, North Carolina. Although the boy wrestled with a stutter through his early years, when he appeared before groups, the stammering receded. Words came easily to him, along with the fire to go with them. Jesse soon became a regular speaker at his church.

He held fast to his religious impulses as a teenager. A childhood friend later remembered Jesse after a football practice telling him that he had already made a decision about his future. He was going to become a minister. On another occasion, he related to Noah Robinson one of his dreams in which he was a preacher leading his followers through raging rivers.

Throughout his life, Robinson was never far from Jesse's thoughts. Even though he never shared his home or lived with him in the same house, Jesse admired his ability to make it against long odds in the white man's world. Calvin Morris, a longtime friend of Jackson's, said, "He often talked about how his father related to white people…the father did not have to grovel. The father had an ability to relate to white people as much as one could be in the segregated South as an equal. He's very appreciative of that in his dad and very proud of his father. And very proud of his father's success."[9]

One of Jesse's early heroes was a minister named James Hall. In October 1959, baseball star Jackie Robinson, who had broken the color barrier in the major leagues a decade earlier, visited Greenville to deliver a speech at a national conference of the National Association for the Advancement of Colored People (NAACP). While Robinson was in the airport, a fracas ensued as airport personnel insisted on observing the segregated "Whites Only" section. Word of the affront to Robinson quickly spread throughout Greenville's black citizenry, and the incident provoked the first major protest march against segregation in the city. The leader of the march was James Hall.

Jesse later remembered, "He was the pastor who first introduced me to social action—Jesus and social change and Mahatma Gandhi.… Pastor

Hall led a march, over much resistance from the community, because they just couldn't understand why a preacher could do such things. He began to interpret the Gospel in a broader application."[10]

Jesse made an impressive mark in his days at Sterling High. He finished 10th in his high school class and was class president, a National Junior Honor Society student, a member of the student council, and state officer of the Future Teachers of America. He starred as quarterback on the Sterling High Tigers football team. It was through his athletic prowess that he began to realize his chance to move out from under the grinding poverty and racial injustice that had so plagued his own family and others of Greenville's black community.

BOTH LEGS AND BRAINS

This was not a potentially great quarterback at the helm for Sterling High. But he had impressive athletic ability, if not a rifle-like arm, and above all, as his coach J. D. Mathis often said, there was a great head above those shoulder pads. He could walk up to the line of scrimmage, look over the defense, spot the weakness in the defensive set, and make the best audible call possible. Also, when pressured, he could get out of trouble with a good set of legs.

Leadership, intelligence, and the stamina and speed to keep moving— that's what Jesse brought to the football field. It was also what he brought to the rest of his life and career. "I'm still playing quarterback," Jackson said later. "I still must look at the defense, strategize and execute with the expectation of success. That's what Coach Mathis taught."[11]

Mathis was a stern disciplinarian, pushing his players mentally and physically on and off the field. His grueling practices at Mayberry Park were legendary. The coach walked the halls of Sterling High to see that his players were in their classes and taking their schoolwork seriously. From this tutelage, Jesse Jackson emerged more confident and resilient. He also came out of his graduation year with a football scholarship to the University of Illinois.

NOTES

1. April E. Moorefield and Dale Perry, "Jackson's Hometown Friends Saddened but Supportive," *Greenville News*, January 18, 2001, http://www.greenville news.com/news/2001/01/18/200101181310.htm.

2. Patricia C. McKissack, *Jesse Jackson: A Biography* (New York: Scholastic, 1989), 4.

3. Moorefield and Perry, "Jackson's Hometown Friends Saddened but Supportive."

4. McKissack, *Jesse Jackson*, 4.

5. Marshall Frady, *Jesse: The Life and Pilgrimage of Jesse Jackson* (New York: Random House, 1996), 76.

6. Frady, *Jesse*, 86.

7. Glenn Arnold, "You Can Pray If You Want To—A 1977 Interview with Jesse Jackson," reprinted in *Christianity Today*, February 8, 2002, http://www.christianitytoday.com/ct/2002/104/51.0.html. Jackson's reference is to the biblical injunction "Cast your bread upon the waters" (Eccl. 1–1). Generosity will be returned.

8. "Jesse Jackson: A Candid Conversation with the Fiery Heir Apparent to Martin Luther King," *Playboy*, November 1969, http://www.geocities.com/heart land/9766/jackson.htm.

9. "Frontline Interview: Calvin Morris," http://www.pbs.org/wgbh/pages/frontline/jesse/interviews/morris.html.

10. Arnold, "You Can Pray If You Want To."

11. "It's Time to Give 'Ol Coach His Due," http://greenvilleonline.com/news/opinion/2004/02/10/2004021024606.htm.

Chapter 3

COLLEGE, JACKIE, AND THE BIRTH OF AN ACTIVIST

Urbana, Illinois, did not turn out to be the Promised Land. With his athletic scholarship in hand Jesse Jackson left the South by train in 1959 for the first time and headed off to a major university. Part of the prestigious Big Ten Conference, the University of Illinois had produced over the years a number of notable football players. Jesse's own expectations and those of his family, friends, and the black community in Greenville were extraordinarily high as he set out to seek his football fortune in this small south-central Illinois town. Those expectations were rudely slapped down in Urbana.

From his earliest days on campus, Jesse seemed out of place and uneasy, his usual ebullience submerged in doubt. He had difficulty making friends and did not fit in with the general manners and culture of the institution, his black, southern ways and manner seemingly ill fitting and mistrusted.

During Christmas break in 1959, Jesse returned to Greenville. While home, he experienced a confrontation that would ultimately prove profound to his own sense of self-respect and in determining the direction in which his life would turn.

To fulfill a school assignment of preparing a speech with annotated references, Jesse entered Greenville's central public library and asked for some books that he could not find in the small segregated library for blacks. He was refused, and some policemen who happened to be in the library at the time threatened him with arrest. The main Greenville library, they reminded the young college freshman, was for whites only.

All the racial humiliations he had suffered through the years, all the pressures of making it out of an urban slum, and all the frustrations and difficulties of coping with his first year at college—all of this tore at his pride. "I walked out front," he remembered later, "and I looked at that sign that said Greenville Public Library and wept."[1]

Jesse's second semester at the University of Illinois proved to be no more successful than the first. As his swagger and confidence sank, so did his grades and his performance on the football field. He was a long way from home in every sense. When he returned to Greenville after the school year, he had already decided not to continue his studies at the University of Illinois. His future direction, he knew, was uncertain. But first he had some unfinished business at the Greenville Public Library.

On July 17, 1960, Jesse, along with three other boys and three girls, walked into the library, sat down inside against the orders of library personnel and the police, were arrested, and were charged with disorderly conduct. They were held for 45 minutes. At her home, Helen Jackson, ironing, saw a news report on her small black-and-white television set and dropped her iron. It was the first time she ever saw her son on television, and he was being released from jail. Neither Jesse nor his mother could have realized at the time that this was the first step in a long personal crusade. He was joining the movement for racial justice.

THE FIGHT FOR CIVIL RIGHTS

Although the practice of human slavery had been ended in the United States by the Civil War, repression of black Americans had become increasingly systematic. As U.S. legislatures and courts found ways to deny blacks the right to vote and other basic freedoms enjoyed by whites, they institutionalized second-class citizenship for dark-skinned individuals.

In 1898, the Supreme Court's *Plessy v. Ferguson* decision legitimized the practice of railroads providing "separate but equal" accommodations for black and white citizens. The case involved Homer Plessy, a black man who, defying the law, sat in the white section of a railroad car. Initially fined $25, Plessy contested the decision all the way to the Supreme Court. The high court upheld the state's "separate but equal" doctrine. It was this decision against which reformers would battle long into the 20th century.

Plessy v. Ferguson led to more than just separate railroad cars. Schools, restaurants, courthouses, bathrooms, and even drinking fountains were also segregated. "Whites Only" signs became common. The law influenced most kinds of interaction between blacks and whites. The decision in 1898 exemplified the race hatred plaguing the country, a time that saw more than 1,000 lynchings in the 1890s and a series of race riots after the turn of the century.

In 1948, the politics of race raised its fierce and ominous form, sparked by two significant developments on the civil rights road. The first was President Harry Truman's decision to integrate the Army. Although blacks had served in the armed forces since the American Revolution, they were, as in other aspects of society, segregated, assigned to all-black, mostly noncombat units. Living in separate barracks, they ate in separate dining halls. Spurred by the performance of black troops in World War II, by the urging of civil rights groups, and by a report issued by a presidential Committee on Civil Rights, Truman issued an executive order. It guaranteed equal treatment for all persons in the armed services regardless of race, color, or national origin.

Also in 1948, a young mayor of Minneapolis, Minnesota, Hubert Humphrey, led liberals in a successful fight at the Democratic Party convention to put a strong civil rights plank in the party platform. Feeling angered and betrayed by the direction of the party, a number of southern delegates rebelled, formed a separate party whose message was simply to denounce race intermingling, called themselves "Dixiecrats," and carried four southern states in the 1948 election.

In 1954, when Jesse Jackson was 13 years old, the U.S. Supreme Court, in the decision *Brown v. Board of Education*, finally struck down the doctrine of "separate but equal," enunciated in the *Plessy v. Ferguson* case at the turn of the century. Black community leaders in Topeka, Kansas, aided by the local chapter of the National Association for the Advancement of Colored People (NAACP), brought suit against the Board of Education of Topeka Schools, arguing that their children were being denied equal education.

On May 17, 1954, the Court, in a unanimous decision, stated that the "separate but equal" clause was unconstitutional because it violated the children's 14th Amendment rights by separating them solely on the classification of the color of their skin. In delivering the Court's opinion, Chief Justice Earl Warren declared, "Segregated schools are not equal and cannot be made equal, and hence they are deprived of the equal protection of the laws." This ruling in favor of integration was one of the most significant strides America ever took in favor of civil liberties.

As the civil rights struggle in these years turned on the fundamental issue of equal treatment and the policies of segregation, a black woman named Rosa Parks, a seamstress for a department store in Montgomery, Alabama, crossed a significant dividing line, and the civil rights movement never looked back. Active in the work of the NAACP, Rosa Parks knew well the Montgomery law requiring blacks to surrender their seats on public buses if segregated white sections were full. Blacks had to pay fares at the front door and then enter the bus at the rear door to avoid contact with white passengers. She was also convinced that any challenge to the law should be done with nonviolence, dignity, and determination.

On December 1, 1955, she boarded the Cleveland Avenue bus and took a seat in the fifth row in front of the "Colored Section." The driver notified the police, who arrested Parks for violating city and state ordinances. Parks was released on $100 bond. Following Parks's arrest, several political activists in the city quickly gave the word to fellow workers to mimeograph thousands of leaflets calling for a boycott of the city buses on Monday, December 5, the day of the scheduled trial of Parks. They also asked a young minister and activist from Atlanta, Martin Luther King Jr., pastor of Dexter Baptist Church, to lead the boycott. Parks pleaded not guilty but was convicted and fined 14 dollars.

Parks's arrest and Martin Luther King's leadership of the Montgomery bus boycott were calls to action, catalysts that would drive the civil rights movement for many years. National attention was now focused on Montgomery and the boycott. From his vantage point in Greenville, Jesse Jackson, now a high school student, began to hear of the protests and of the name of Martin Luther King Jr.

King soon became an internationally recognized figure not only for his stand on equal rights but also for his insistence on nonviolent protest. Despite several bombings of the homes of black leaders in Montgomery, including that of King himself, the civil rights leader had maintained a dignified yet forceful crusader, his eloquent oratory filling halls, churches, and auditoriums throughout the American South and beyond.

King and his followers fought intimidation and violence with resolve and economic power. The boycott forced compromise. The nonviolent marches and protests raised the cause of equal rights to communities far outside the American South. In the next few years, King led other bus boycotts, made speeches around the country, and led demonstrations—and he was sometimes arrested. It was all part of an evolving strategy of nonviolent protest.

Black students started "sit-ins" at lunch counters in the South. If they weren't served, they wouldn't leave. The sit-ins spread to various cities. Many of the students were jailed.

In February 1960, in Greensboro, North Carolina, four black students staged a sit-in at the lunch counter at the downtown Woolworth's store. They were from North Carolina A&T, a predominantly black college. Watching the television reports from Urbana was Jesse Jackson, homesick for the South and beginning to take an interest in the growing storm over civil rights.

FINDING THE PLACE

In September 1960, Jesse transferred from the University of Illinois to North Carolina A&T. Arriving on campus without a scholarship and also without money, he talked his way into school. With his cockiness and confidence apparently rejuvenated on returning to the South, young Jackson visited the public affairs office, the registrar's office, and finally the president of North Carolina A&T, Samuel Proctor, in a zealous campaign to convince the school that Jesse Jackson belonged on campus. Proctor, a highly respected African American minister, college professor, civil rights activist, and writer, later wrote of Jackson, "He was adventurous enough to try anything…and opted to come to us, with no money and ineligible for an athletic scholarship, pleading to be admitted. Even in his interviews he was so impressive that we made some very special arrangements to have him admitted. We never regretted it."[2]

Although Jesse had felt mired in disappointment and regret at the University of Illinois, he flourished at North Carolina A&T. In a familiar southern atmosphere, he felt a resurgence of enthusiasm and camaraderie with his fellow students and assumed again, as he had in high school, a place of leadership. He studied hard and played hard. He became an honor student and, although not destined for sports greatness, starred as quarterback on the football team. He joined the Omega Psi Phi fraternity and was elected to a national position in the organization.

He breezily moved through the university's social scene, rounding up friends and acquaintances like a western herder on an open range. He gave public speeches and showed up at Proctor's lectures and sermons, always making it a point to congratulate the university president after his presentation. So direct was his earnestness and eager advances that some found Jackson annoying and overbearing. But most who spent time with Jackson recognized his obvious strengths and talents and held him in high regard. At this university, the kid from Greenville was something of a prince in the making.

JACKIE

One rainy afternoon in the fall semester of 1961 at North Carolina A&T, an attractive 18-year-old freshman majoring in sociology and psychology was scurrying toward the Student Union Building. To get there, she hurried through the members of the football team gathered along the sidewalk. Suddenly, one of the players yelled at her, "Hey girl, I'm going to marry you."[3] Startled, she turned to see which one of the players had made the unexpected remark, stepped in a puddle of water, and soaked her suede shoes. The player was Jesse Jackson.

Obviously unnerved by the comment, Jackie Brown walked a little more quickly toward the Student Union. In the days following, she did what she could to stay a distance from A&T's quarterback.

Jackie was the oldest of five children of a single mother and teenage migrant worker from Fort Pierce, Florida, who picked fruit and vegetables for 15 cents a bushel in the sand and sweltering humidity of Florida's fields. When Jackie's mother married a man from Newport News, Virginia, she was so uncertain of her future that she decided to leave Jackie to be cared for by a friend in the migrant worker camp. Later, when the friend passed away, she brought Jackie to Newport News. As was the case with Jesse Jackson, life's beginnings for Jackie Brown could have hardly been less humble. But she had, as Jackson, through grit, talent, and energy, made it to college at North Carolina A&T.

Vivacious, adventuresome, with a mixture of frivolity and serious purpose, Jackie Brown partied and mixed easily with fellow students but, at the same time, became so engrossed in intellectual and spiritual interests that, for a time, she had even considered becoming a nun. Her early youth in the migrant worker camps and the social evils she had found firsthand translated into a genuine passion for social change. She wanted to make a difference.

She read about the Cuban revolution and the expressed aims of its leaders to make life easier for the underclasses. She engaged friends in talking about the civil rights protest movement gaining momentum after Rosa Parks's courageous action in 1955. She idolized strong women in American history, such as the abolitionist Sojourner Truth and First Lady and UN Ambassador Eleanor Roosevelt.

As Jesse ignored Jackie's attempts to avoid him and as she heard others rave about his looks and his talent, the barrier she had built began quickly to topple. Soon, everything about Jesse Jackson seemed to interest Jackie, from his background and interests, so similar to her own, to his energy and intelligence.

He seemed unlike anyone she had ever met. They talked about U.S. foreign policy, about race relations and Jesse's growing admiration for Dr. Martin Luther King Jr., and even about religion. During this early stage of their relationship, she was more politically radical than he. They argued and matched wits. Jesse insisted that they attend church services every Sunday morning; she balked.

At times he infuriated her with his aggressive attempts to control her. At other times, he resorted to old-fashioned approaches. He brought pies from home baked by his mother. He marched over to her dorm with a contingent of fellow fraternity members to sing Smokey Robinson songs under her window. Gradually, the attraction was mutual.

On New Year's Eve 1962, Jesse and Jackie exchanged wedding vows in his family's home in Greenville. She wore a gown she had made herself from eggshell-colored silk. Reverend D. S. Sample of Long Branch Baptist Church performed the service.

When she looked back years later to her decision to marry Jesse Jackson, Jackie talked about her realization that this man could make a profound difference not only in her life but also in the larger society. She talked about the debt they both owed to those who brought them through their early years to be in a position to advance. "We were given an opportunity to make a difference in the world," she said. "We are to bring things back to the community or create a new community. That was our responsibility and obligation when we left home. To bring something big back. Something new and you're to be a better person when you return." Her alliance with Jesse, she believed, could make it possible. "You're supposed to change and make things better for other people. Those who are back home. How could we do that? We had to join with people and forces who were making a change."[4]

In July 1963, Jackie gave birth to their first child, a daughter they named Santita. Jackie and Jesse decided that she should leave North Carolina A&T to care for the child and help support the family. Within two years, the couple had two boys, Jesse Louis, born in 1965, and Jonathan Luther, born in 1966. In 1970, their fourth child, a boy they named Yusef Dubois, was born and in 1975 their fifth child, Jacqueline Lavinia.

FOR THE MOVEMENT

As Jesse progressed at North Carolina A&T, Samuel Proctor, the university president, became a close mentor. In his youth a fellow student of Martin Luther King at Boston University, now an influential civil rights spokesman, Proctor increasingly saw in Jackson a young warrior for the cause. He recognized Jesse's growing admiration for King and understood that in Jackson he had a student of intellectual promise and indomitable energy.

Proctor counseled Jesse to model his own career after that of King, whose civil rights movement rested on both an intellectual and a religious grounding. King was familiar with the great philosophical and religious thinkers, appreciated the lessons of history, and marched to a deep sense of calling. At the core of King's work was a resiliency of faith and religious commitment anchored on solid intellectual ground. In Jesse, Proctor saw the closest young facsimile of King on the movement's horizon. Proctor prodded Jesse to consider graduate studies after completing his degree at North Carolina A&T.

At this point, aside from his own protest at the library in Greenville, Jesse had not joined the other A&T students in their continuing civil rights demonstrations but had remained in the background, uncertain of the kind of role he should play. He had attended a meeting of the campus chapter of the Congress of Racial Equality (CORE), a civil rights organization active since the 1940s in pushing for social change on the race issue. He had voiced support for its work, and became a member. Finally, when a number of the student leaders decided to ask Jesse to take a leadership position, he agreed. He would lead sit-ins and marches. He would put himself and his future on the line for a just cause.

Proctor gave him advice that Jesse would remember as pivotal: "So, if you are as committed as you say you are, you must decide now to be a student of the movement, not just a student in the movement. You will cease to be a student at some point, and so your commitment to the struggle must be your commitment to prepare to offer something of substance to it."[5]

Jesse and his troops conducted "watch-ins" at theaters, "eat-ins" at restaurants, and "wade-ins" at swimming pools. They marched and mobilized and stirred others into action. Recognizing Jesse's leadership qualities, his fellow students at A&T elected him president of the North Carolina Intercollegiate Council on Human Rights, a newly formed organization designed to coordinate student civil rights protests in the state. Jesse was also elected president of the student body.

In May 1963, at about the same time a large civil rights march was under way in Birmingham, Alabama, Jackson and other young civil rights activists of CORE, engaged in major antisegregation protest marches in front of Greensboro's stores and theaters. Taking a cue from the tactics of Dr. King—nonviolent protest within the context of religious and moral values—Jackson became increasingly inventive and his oratory ever-more colorful, persuasive, and enlivened by snippets of rhyme. At one of the early rallies, he exclaimed, "Demonstrations without hestitations. Jail without bail."[6]

During one demonstration outside a cafeteria, he recalled later, "police finally were moving to arrest us, and we kneeled and started saying the Lord's Prayer. Police all took off their caps and bowed their heads. Can't arrest folks prayin'. We finished, they started for us again. We stood up and started singing 'The Star-Spangled Banner.' They stopped, put their hands over their heart. Can't arrest folks singing the national anthem. We were touching something bigger, see, that we both respected. Opening up the moral terms of the situation. Went on for, like, half an hour, until we got tired and let 'em arrest us."[7]

In late May 1963, nearly a thousand students from North Carolina A&T, joined by a number of white students from nearby Guilford College, marched into downtown Greensboro and took up places in front of the S & W Cafeteria, the Mayfair Cafeteria, the Center Theater, and the Carolina Theater. They demanded an end to segregation in all of Greensboro's commercial establishments.

The demonstrators promised to fill the jails unless their demands were met. The police quickly obliged. Both the county and the city jails filled up with college students. More than 1,400 students were arrested within six days.

When law enforcement needed additional detention space, they turned to an abandoned polio hospital. Dilapidated, with far less space than necessary to house the growing number of demonstrators, the building soon became a sweltering prison chamber for the students crammed inside, panting for air. As Jackson listened to their yells, amidst the police with their dogs and the marchers, Jesse began to deliver a spontaneous but eloquent plea for justice for the protesters and their cause. His face glistening with perspiration and tears, Jackson, without notes of any kind, reached an inspired level that astonished even some of his friends.

From what well of creativity did the words come—so quickly, so powerfully? One of his friends later asked Jesse if he could have a copy of the speech to use for organizing work in future demonstrations. Jesse could not even remember what he had said. It had all come from within, he said. It was at the time of this speech and the atmosphere surrounding it, Jackson recalled later, that he began to recognize himself the magnificence of the oratorical gift he had been given—this power to raise people's hopes and make them feel better about themselves and lead them to a cause. He could poetically summon words and phrases, marshal arguments, and call for action as few orators before or after. He could never explain the gift to himself or others; he just had it.

Jesse looked back to the speech in Greensboro as a turning point in his life. This fight for justice, this role as an agent for change, he began to realize, would be his life's work. And most who knew Jackson well believed that whatever road he chose, he would run on that road with much vigor. His mentor Samuel DeWitt Proctor wrote, "He was aggressive and bodacious, but he matched it with intelligence and purpose. Whatever he said, or did, he was usually right and reasonable."[8]

As the protests in Greensboro continued, organizers, led by the national director of CORE, James Farmer, threatened a boycott of those businesses that continued to refuse service to black citizens. Jesse himself was finally jailed. At one of the marches, he simply asked the group to lie down in the middle of one of the city's main streets. He was charged with inciting a riot.

Back in Greenville, Jesse's mother at first recoiled when she heard the news of her son's arrest. Later, she said, "Since then I just saw he had his mind made up to go on with it. And you know that boy is a powerful figure, he's God-given, and I'm just real proud of him."[9]

Reverend Richard Hicks, minister of the Trinity African Methodist Episcopal Zion Church, emphasized at one of the rallies just how serious and determined the protesters were in taking on the establishment. "This boycott is no child's play," he exclaimed. "This is war. This is a revolution."[10]

It was a war that the demonstrators in Greensboro would win. By the end of the protests, the city mayor had persuaded local businesses to open their doors to blacks. Segregation by merchants, at least in Greensboro, had been broken, and Jesse Jackson had played a pivotal role in making it happen.

When Jackie Jackson later looked back on those days, she said of her husband, "He took on his own identity in Greensboro and from there he was made a man and able to move forward and do what he is doing today. Working with people and uplifting and changing the quality of the life for most people. A fire was already lit from Greenville, but he began to live, he became a man in Greensboro. It is my opinion."[11]

IN THE IMAGE OF KING

On August 28, 1963, approximately a quarter of a million individuals gathered at the Lincoln Memorial in Washington, D.C. From all parts of the United States and abroad, they came to call for a redress of grievances against black Americans. They, along with millions of viewers of televisions across the world, heard Reverend Martin Luther King Jr., many for the first time. They heard him deliver in thunderous and moving images his "I Have a Dream" speech, his vision of what the United States could be—a nation in which all citizens were measured by their character, not by the color of their skin.

In the throng that day was Samuel Proctor, a close friend of King's who had been Jesse's mentor at North Carolina A&T. It was Proctor who had long conversations with Jesse about the power of the gospel to achieve social change and about the example set by King, who was essentially a religious leader.

Jesse was also in Washington on that day. "I remember listening with tears in my eyes to the great words of Martin Luther King, who transcended on that day all categories, blending the spiritual and the political and the economic."[12]

The protests and marches in the summer of 1963 and the March on Washington transformed the civil rights movement. Thousands of formerly segregated schools, restaurants, hotels, parks, and lunch counters now served black Americans along with whites. Many companies added blacks to their workforces. President John F. Kennedy asked Congress for a civil rights bill to end segregation. Most important, black Americans experienced a birth of feeling about their own value, a pride in their culture, and new hope for the future.

In the spring of 1964, Jackson received a bachelor of arts degree from North Carolina A&T. By the time of his graduation, he had decided to follow the example of Martin Luther King Jr. With his considerable talents, especially his intellect and oratorical skills, Jackson could have chosen a number of career paths—politics, social service, or the law. Instead, as had King, Jackson decided to follow the ministry. With a grant from the Rockefeller Foundation, he enrolled in a graduate program at the Chicago Theological Seminary. He would become a preacher and an evangelist for social change.

NOTES

1. Glenn Arnold, "You Can Pray If You Want To—A 1977 Interview with Jesse Jackson," reprinted in *Christianity Today*, February 8, 2002, http://www.christianitytoday.com/ct/2002/104/51.0.html.

2. Samuel Proctor, *The Substance of Things Hoped For* (New York: G. P. Putnam's Sons, 1996), 97.

3. "Frontline: The Long Pilgrimage of Jesse Jackson: Jackie Jackson Interview," http://www.pbs.org/wgbh/pages/frontline/jesse/interviews/jackie.html.

4. "Frontline."

5. "Interview with Rev. Jesse Jackson, Civil Rights Leader," http://www.teen ink.com/Past/9900/January/Interview.

6. Marshall Frady, *Jesse: The Life and Pilgrimage of Jesse Jackson* (New York: Random House, 1996), 173.

7. Marshall Frady, "Greensboro Sit-Ins: Launch of a Civil Rights Movement," http://www.greensboro.com/sitins/960621.htm.

8. Proctor, *The Substance of Things Hoped For*, 109.

9. "Emerging Rights Leader," *New York Times*, May 24, 1968.

10. *New York Times*, May 21, 1963.

11. "Frontline."

12. Jesse Jackson, "40 Years Later...Have We Overcome Yet?," *Ebony*, August 2003, 165.

Chapter 4

JOINING THE
KING MOVEMENT

CHICAGO THEOLOGICAL SEMINARY

Jackson, along with Jackie and the new baby, Santita, motored all the way from the South to Chicago in the late summer of 1964, in an old white Corvair, pulling a U-Haul. Arriving on a dreary day, as he sat down on the side of the bed in their room, Jackson realized that this was a significant moment in his life. Jackie was expecting a second child, and the pressures of a growing family meant increasing responsibility. But he now believed that his religious and social service mission was now before him. His direction was clear, and he was determined to make a difference.

As he prepared to take on his graduate work at Chicago Theological Seminary, he desperately needed a job. For a short time, he worked for Mayor Richard J. Daley as an apprentice in one of the precincts of Chicago's South Side, an area in the city to which many of the blacks had migrated from southern states over the years. The South Side was now one of many areas involved in Mayor Daley's infamous political machine that relied on small favors for votes.

But when Daley asked Jesse to take a job as a toll collector in the transit system, Jackson, considering the job an insult to his background and qualifications, was infuriated. He left Daley's employ.

He soon landed a job working as a salesman for John Johnson, the black publisher who owned both *Jet* and *Ebony* magazines. Jessie's job was to sell the publications to the newsstands. In the inner-city black wards of Chicago, Jesse was now doing what he did best—communicating. It was during these early days in Chicago that Jackson began to learn the inside workings of those neighborhoods of Chicago that he would influence so profoundly in the coming years.

Jackson worked hard at his seminary studies, at first keeping a distance from the local civil rights organizations, many of which were trying to recruit him as a potential leader. He did work with Chicago's Coordinating Council of Community Organizations, an umbrella group for civic and civil rights organizations, serving as director of field activities from 1965 to 1966.

But his studies remained his highest priority during that first year in Chicago. Jackson later recalled that Professor Ross Snyder, who taught Christian education, helped him think outside the narrow confines of religious training. For the student activist, this message of connecting God's word to the problems of social dislocation and the challenges of community building was not only instructive but also relevant to the kind of calling that Jackson saw ahead in his life. "I had a certain certainty about God," Jackson recalled, "but at CTS they took God out of the box, and that took me to some strange places."[1]

Jackson said that Snyder especially encouraged students to look inward for spirituality and strength. In addition, at the seminary, Jackson read many of the texts of Paul Tillich and other theologians and the writings of Mahatma Gandhi that had so informed another man of God who was turning his strength to social action—Martin Luther King Jr.

KING

Born on January 15, 1929, Martin Luther King Jr. was 12 years older than Jackson but only a few years younger than Jackson's mother. Even before he had actually met King, Jackson had begun to embrace him as a strong role model, and, as many of King and Jackson's friends later recalled, Jesse would soon begin to see in the older man something of a father figure. Andrew Young, a minister, human rights activist, and colleague of King who was in his career a congressman, ambassador to the United Nations, and mayor of Atlanta, knew well the relationship between King and Jackson. Young said, "I always suspected that Jesse's childhood as the son of a single mother created in him a constant psychological need for a father figure."[2]

King's background was markedly different from that of Jesse. When King was born on January 15, 1929, it was in an upstairs bedroom of an impressive Victorian home in the section of Atlanta, Georgia, known as "Sweet Auburn," the heart of the black community. He was the son of the Reverend Martin Luther King Sr., highly respected pastor of Ebenezer Baptist Church, located two blocks east of the house on Auburn Avenue. King's grandfather also held a pastorate in Ebenezer Baptist Church. For the first 12 years of his life, King took in the atmosphere of a large family, including aunts, uncles, parents, and grandparents and the vibrancy surrounding an active Church life—the powerful sermons on Sunday mornings, the rousing music, and the emphasis on learning and intellectual exploring imparted by those around him.

It was no surprise that King, following in the footsteps of his father and grandfather, was ordained in the Christian ministry at Ebenezer Baptist in 1948, at the age of 19, and became assistant pastor.

After attending Morehouse College in Atlanta, a highly respected all-black school, King went on to study at Crozer Theological Seminary in Pennsylvania and Boston University. He received a Ph.D. in systematic theology in 1955.

After his studies, King returned again to the South, accepting the pastorate of the Dexter Avenue Baptist Church in Montgomery, Alabama. It was in Montgomery, where Rosa Parks refused to sit at the back of a bus and thus launched the bus boycott, that King became a central leader in the civil rights movement. As president of the Montgomery Improvement Association and leader of the boycott that lasted throughout 1956, King gained national prominence.

In December 1956, the U.S. Supreme Court declared Alabama's segregation laws unconstitutional, and Montgomery buses were desegregated. The decision was a milestone in the civil rights movement and one of many of Martin Luther King Jr.'s towering achievements.

The Supreme Court decision fueled the passion and determination of King and his followers. In 1957, they formed the Southern Christian Leadership Conference (SCLC). The bus desegregation success proved that nonviolent direct action could succeed. Embodying the vision and philosophy of King, the SCLC fostered a mass movement based on the Christian tenets of love and understanding and became a major force in American politics. King and other SCLC leaders were indefatigable in rallying town after town and community after community to accept their strategy of confronting government and business power with nonviolent methods; to take on the always discouraging odds for the cause of racial justice and civil rights; to put behind them the taunts and threats of the mobs, the small defeats, and the large setbacks; and to keep on working, and singing and marching. From one town to another, from one set of circumstances to another, they challenged the power with marches, boycotts, and sit-ins. They took on southern racism in an orderly, structured, and peaceful series of campaigns.

Later in 1957, King resigned from Dexter Avenue Baptist Church and returned to his home in Atlanta. He became copastor of Ebenezer Baptist Church with his father. From this base in Atlanta, he would run the operations of the SCLC.

Through the early years of the 1960s, King and his organization sponsored various sit-in movements to push for integration. In the spring of 1963, at about the same time Jackson, while a student at North Carolina A&T, was first joining the sit-in movements in Greensboro, North Carolina, King and SCLC were leading mass demonstrations in Birmingham, Alabama. It was in Birmingham where the name of Eugene "Bull" Connor, the chief of police, became closely linked with attack dogs and fire hoses, which he used on unarmed black protestors. Those dogs and those streams of water that knocked over scores of men, women, and children on the streets of Birmingham once again proved the efficacy of King's strategy of nonviolent confrontation. Despite the pain and injuries and overwhelming indignities suffered, the protestors prevailed. Their campaigns resulted in desegregated restrooms, drinking fountains, and lunch counters in Birmingham and an agreement by business leaders to hire and promote more black employees. Responding to the Birmingham protests, President John F. Kennedy submitted broad civil rights legislation to Congress, which eventually led to the passage of the Civil Rights Act of 1964.

By August 1963, when Jackson traveled to Washington to see King's "I Have a Dream" speech on the steps of the Lincoln Memorial, the civil rights leader had gained international fame. He was awarded the Nobel Peace Prize in 1964. Accepting the award for peace on behalf of the civil rights movement, he declared that "nonviolence is the answer to the crucial political and moral question of our time—the need for man to overcome oppression and violence without resorting to violence and oppression."[3]

SELMA

On March 7, 1965, a day that would become known in civil rights history as "Bloody Sunday," some 600 civil rights demonstrators marched east out of Selma, Alabama, on U.S. Route 80 toward Montgomery, the state capital, to petition Governor George Wallace. The demand was for the right of black Alabamans to vote.

The marchers got only as far as the Edmund Pettus Bridge six blocks away, where they were met by state and local lawmen wearing gas masks and carrying billy clubs, some riding on horseback and flailing whips, and others wielding electric cattle prods. They beat and gassed the marchers as along the sides of the road many whites cheered on the attack.

The televised images from Alabama shocked the nation. Sitting in living rooms all over America, viewers could see black demonstrators attempting to protest peacefully being attacked by fellow Americans. They could see the racial hate and resentment, built from generations, that was ignited and on full display. It brought to full view the kind of brutality that made the stories about lynchings and murders and the power of the Ku Klux Klan seem more immediate to Americans. These images of blood-streaked demonstrators in Selma helped rally support for the 1965 Voting Rights Act.

The "Bloody Sunday" confrontation prompted King to call for clergy members nationwide to come to Selma. One of the viewers that day was a divinity student in Chicago. As he watched on late-night television the accounts of the demonstrations and the violence from Alabama and as he heard the pleas from the organizers for help from others around the country, Jackson decided to act. At the time, Jackie, along with Santita, was in Greenville, South Carolina, with her family awaiting the birth of the Jackson's second child.

The next day, standing on a table in the school cafeteria, Jackson began to challenge the students to join him in making a statement on behalf of their own institution. If the seminary stood for discipleship, what better witness could they make than to join in this protest of conscience? By the time he was finished recruiting, around 20 fellow students and five professors, most of them white, joined Jackson in a caravan headed to Alabama. They included the highly respected Alvin Pitcher, a longtime white civil rights worker and professor at the University of Chicago's Divinity School.

On March 9, King led a second march. This time, 1,500 strong crossed the bridge before meeting up with the troopers on the other side. After King led the marchers in prayer, he asked them to turn back to avoid further violence. They did. Nevertheless, that night James Reeb, a white Unitarian-Universalist minister from Boston who had arrived to join the march, was clubbed in Selma. He died three days later. Reeb was the second protestor to be killed in Selma. Jimmie Lee Jackson, a black hospital worker, had been shot and killed by a state trooper while trying to protect his mother and grandfather, who were being beaten during an earlier voter registration march.

When Jackson arrived in Selma with his group of students and professors, Andrew Young, one of King's closest confidants, quickly recognized
the fire in Jackson from the first time he saw him. He saw how Jackson
not only eagerly accepted responsibility but also went out of his way to assume it. "One night after the terrible attack at the Edmund Pettis Bridge,"
Young later recalled, "members of the SCLC staff were monitoring bar-
ricades outside the Brown Chapel AME [African Methodist Episcopal]
Church. By that time, most of us had gone several days without rest. Jesse
volunteered to monitor the situation, saying, 'You all go relax. I'll keep
watch here for you.'"[4]

Young remembered thinking that it was quite remarkable that Jackson
swept into a terribly intense situation with such coolness. Surrounded by
the police with their dogs barking, the crowds shouting and confusion
everywhere, Jackson moved to the front. "Well, in that kind of situation,
taking charge meant being thrown in jail, it meant getting beaten up. It
was less than a week since the Reverend James Reeb had been beaten to
death about three blocks from where we were standing. So is this guy for
real? Is he really courageous? Or does he just not know any better. And I
decided that here was a natural-born leader. And he just couldn't stand in
line with everybody else."[5]

Young spoke of Jackson's air of confidence far beyond his experience.
He also saw that, unlike many of the younger protestors, Jackson's sense
of mission was undergirded by religious impulse. Like several of the older
leaders of the movement, he was a passionate but levelheaded young man
with obvious leadership qualities of the first order.

Hours after his arrival in Selma, he was scurrying around volunteering
for this assignment or that. If he had no assignment, he would begin to
give assignments to others. He gave impromptu speeches. He met King's
lieutenant Ralph Abernathy and then King himself. He talked with King
about the possibility of helping the movement in Chicago.

In the midst of this major civil rights event, those around him could see
the raw energy at work. He could whip up a crowd with stirring rhetoric
laced with biblical references about as well as any of the other ministers.
Although King and the others at first did not know quite what to make
of Jackson, their eyes were wide open as the young student from Chicago
made himself a presence through sheer will.

Roger Wilkins, another civil rights leader, remembers seeing Jackson
for the first time in Selma: "It was in the week between the beatings of
the marchers on the Edmond Prettis bridge when the first march had first
kicked off. I had heard about Jackson. I was in the Justice Department at

the time. And he was already becoming a name in the movement. So I wanted to see him. Curious about him. And, all I really remember was a large human being, and a large presence with enormous energy. Kind of exhorting and moving around and drawing a lot of attention. I was there only briefly. But the impression is very strong."[6]

Betty Washington, a reporter for the black newspaper *Chicago Daily Defender*, remembered gathering around Brown Chapel in Selma while Reverend Abernathy and others gave speeches. Suddenly, "up popped Jesse, wearing an odd-looking porkpie hat and rugged work clothes, and, of course, closely cropped hair. I thought it strange that he would be making a speech, when he was not on the SCLC staff...he just seemed to have come from nowhere."[7] He had not been invited to speak; almost everyone in the crowd had no idea who he was. Yet he seized the moment and the opportunity and performed with such flair and impassioned oratory that many took notice.

Ralph Abernathy, King's principal lieutenant, was particularly impressed and encouraged him to ask Jackson to join the staff of the SCLC. King, who had himself received an honorary doctor of divinity degree from Chicago Theological Seminary in 1957, was also impressed with Jackson, even though he was initially reluctant to hire him because of his youth and inexperience. However, as Abernathy and others spoke about Jackson's work in Selma and his seemingly limitless energy, King became increasingly convinced that he needed him on the team.

Jackson and his squadron from Chicago Theological Seminary needed to head back north before the final march from Selma to Montgomery, but he and the others had fulfilled their personal missions of bearing witness to the cause. For Jackson, now, the image of Martin Luther King Jr. and his moral crusade was riveted in his thoughts. He wanted to be a warrior for the movement.

As the caravan from Chicago passed through Birmingham, Jackson stopped briefly at a gas station phone booth to call his student quarters about any news from South Carolina. There was great news. Jackie had successfully delivered their second child, a boy. They decided to call him Jesse Jr.

After Jackson and the others from the seminary left Selma, the SCLC successfully petitioned a federal district judge for an order barring police from interfering with another march to Montgomery. More than 3,000 people, including a core of 300 marchers who would make the entire trip, left Selma on March 21. They were accompanied by federal marshals and FBI agents dispatched to Alabama by President Lyndon B. Johnson.

The marchers walked 12 miles a day and slept in fields. By the time they reached the state capital on March 25, they numbered about 25,0000.

At the Alabama state capitol building, King led a delegation that handed a petition to Governor George Wallace demanding voting rights for blacks.

Before thousands of onlookers, King declared, "There never was a moment in American history more honorable and more inspiring than the pilgrimage of clergymen and laymen of every race and faith pouring into Selma to face danger at the side of its embattled Negroes."[8]

That night the celebration of victory was shattered by renewed violence. Viola Liuzzo, a white medical lab technician from Michigan who had traveled to Alabama for the march, was shot and killed by Ku Klux Klan members while she was traveling in a car headed back to Selma.

On August 6, 1965, President Johnson signed the Voting Rights Act of 1965. The act banned the use of literacy or other voter qualification tests that had sometimes been used to prevent blacks from voting. The legislation thus empowered the federal government to register those whom the states refused to put on voting lists.

PREPARING TO SERVE

When Jackson arrived back at the apartment in Chicago, he was emotionally exhilarated but physically exhausted and suffering from pneumonia. Jackie, accompanied by their newborn son, Jesse Jr., soon traveled from Greenville to care for him.

Although Jackson was now certain he wanted to work for King, he had as yet no firm offer. He had talked briefly with several of King's lieutenants and with King himself about the possibility of the movement opening a front in Chicago.

On his return, Jackson began a whirlwind tour of the city, visiting prominent religious leaders and social workers about the possibility of a King operation in Chicago. The reception was notably cool. Most of the leaders were intimately tied up with the political machine of Mayor Daley and not anxious to open a rift with the power structure. But Jackson persevered, allying himself with a number of ministers and others who showed a willingness to participate.

But time for Jackson was critical. With a growing family and without a job, the family's finances were nearly at ground zero. At one point during this period, Jackson showed up at his church's weekly food line for groceries.

Finally, about six months after his trip to Selma, Jackson got word from King that he wanted him on the team. King was attracted not only to the passion of this young theology student who had shown up in Alabama for the march earlier that year but to his organizing skills as well.

King was so impressed with the student activist that he asked him to join the movement as a full-time organizer. "You will learn more from working with me in six months than in six years at seminary," King told Jackson.[9]

King recognized early on Jackson's enormous gifts. Although as the relationship developed, the mentor would worry about the student's impatience and ambition and would chafe at his self-promotion, King understood the passion that lay behind the bravado. He knew that Jackson would help bring enormous talent to the SCLC. At age 24, he would be the youngest member of the staff of the SCLC.

When King asked Jackson to join him, the Jackson household exploded with joy. Jackie Jackson remembered that her husband was "overwhelmed." "He was deeply moved by Dr. King. He was deeply moved and it changed his life.... Things changed as of that day. He wanted to work with him. He had talked with him. And he felt that this was a rare opportunity that he would have to work closely with Dr. King and he had already accepted. He did not, there wasn't any delay in, I'll talk it over, let me think about it. He accepted it. And he began immediately to think about things he could do to help him."[10]

Jackson signed on with King and never returned to finish his degree. King appointed Jackson to head the Chicago branch of Operation Breadbasket, the SCLC's effort to deal with the business community in promoting jobs for blacks, a campaign tried earlier in Philadelphia. His job would be to use his considerable talents of persuasion and then, if necessary, to take tactical action, such as community boycotts of targeted businesses.

He was on the move now. One week he was in a church food line, the next he had a position in the organization run by the man he idolized. Jesse Jackson's life kept gaining steam.

NOTES

1. James M. Wall, "Jackson Closes a Chapter," *Christian Century*, June 21, 2000, 667.

2. Andrew Young, *An Easy Burden: The Civil Rights Movement and the Transformation of America* (New York: HarperPerennial, 1996), 386.

3. "The Nobel Peace Prize 1964: Acceptance Speech," http://www.nobel.se/peace/laureates/1964/king-acceptance.html.

4. Young, *An Easy Burden*, 386.

5. "Frontline Interview: Andrew Young," http://www.pbs.org/wgbh/pages/frontline/jesse/interviews/young.html.

6. "Frontline Interview: Roger Wilkins," http://www.pbs.org/wgbh/pages/frontline/jesse/interviews/wilkins.html.

7. Thomas Landess and Richard Quinn, *Jesse Jackson and the Politics of Race* (Ottawa, Ill.: Jameson Books, 1985), 17–18.

8. "Martin Luther King Speech, March 25, 1965," http://www.spartacus.schoolnet.co.uk/USAselma.htm.

9. Wall, "Jackson Closes a Chapter," 667.

10. "Frontline Interview: Jackie Jackson," http://www.pbs.org/wgbh/pages/frontline/jesse/interviews/jackie.html.

Chapter 5

OPERATION BREADBASKET

The Southern Christian Leadership Council (SCLC) gave Jackson his entry into the world of big-time civil rights protest. As the umbrella embracing Martin Luther King Jr.'s belief that nonviolent civil disobedience, as taught by Indian pacifist Mahatma Gandhi and others around the world, could help end segregation and foster social justice for blacks, the organization drew together religious leaders who were committed to community service. In his early writings, King himself had emphasized the extended role of the church and religious impulse in society. If the Christian religion professed the redemption of the soul, it must also be concerned with the economic and social conditions that can scar that soul. Religion, he taught, must be concerned with life on earth as well as life in the hereafter. The Christian religion, he believed, must accept the role of granting help, assistance, and equal opportunity to every individual.

Although King personally dominated the organization, other activists were also prominent. They included Ralph Abernathy, a Baptist minister who was King's closest associate; Andrew Young of the National Council of Churches who later became U.S. ambassador to the United Nations and mayor of Atlanta; Ella Baker, a longtime promoter of community-based civil rights activism from Georgia; and James Bevel, a Navy veteran and student at the Baptist Seminary who had also embraced Gandhi's nonviolent teachings with fierce allegiance.

Working primarily in the South, as the name of the organization implied, the SCLC conducted leadership training programs, citizen education projects, and voter registration drives. The organization played a major part in the civil rights March on Washington, D.C., in 1963 and in antidiscrimination and voter registration drives, notably at Albany, Georgia, and Birmingham and Selma, Alabama, where Jackson first met many of the leaders. Now, however, by the mid-1960s, King turned his attention to the more basic aspects of life in the ghetto. King was determined to conduct campaigns to improve the economic lives of blacks and other minorities and broaden the organization's civil rights agenda by focusing on issues related to poverty.

King had seen the success in the early 1960s of the efforts of civil rights activist Leon Sullivan in Philadelphia. Reverend Sullivan began a program of community self-help and empowerment, based on ideas of nonviolence and direct action. Like King, Sullivan had learned the concepts of Gandhi in his graduate studies. His operation in Philadelphia, called "Selective Patronage," sought to boycott companies that did not offer employment to black men and women. With Sullivan's work as a model, King decided to engage the SCLC in their own efforts at "selective buying campaigns," first in some selected cities in the South and later in the North.

The program would be called Operation Breadbasket, and it would immerse Jackson in major civil rights activity, challenge his organizational acumen, and provide an opportunity for the young activist to show King, his fellow members of the SCLC, and people across the nation just what kind of leadership skills he possessed.

Jackson listened hard to King's advice, accepted most of his political and theological views as his own, modeled his career after that of King, struggled for his attention and approval, and chafed at his rebuffs. He would gradually earn the reputation as the one member of the King organization with the personality, intellect, and magnetism to succeed his teacher.

Calvin Morris, a friend of Jackson's in these years, said that it was clear he had a sense of destiny, a belief that his life would have an effect on society. He understood the powerful relationship between the black church and the black community and the great influence and leadership status that individuals such as Martin Luther King and Andrew Young were having, ministers whose goals were nothing less than to make profound change in American society. Morris remained astonished throughout the years by Jackson's energy. "Jesse has an engine that knows no rest," Morris said. "I have never met a person who can be on 20 hours of the day. And crash 4 hours, put the world aside for 4 hours, wake up, and is about moving and doing and putting things together the next 20."[1]

The aim of Operation Breadbasket was based on simple but effective tactical persuasion. In order to increase the number of jobs for low-income black Americans, the organization would threaten to undertake a boycott on businesses that did not cooperate in the program. If the business did not comply, the boycotts would go forward. As King said, the logic behind such efforts is "if you respect my dollar, you must respect my person" and that Negroes "will no longer spend our money where we cannot get substantial jobs."[2]

In April 1966, from his Operation Breadbasket office in a small South Side house, Jackson launched his first salvo in the campaign to bring greater economic and consumer power to the black community. The first target was a dairy that serviced more than 100 outlets in the black areas of Chicago. After Jackson's request to examine the employment rolls of the company was rejected, a team of pastors from black churches, brought together by Jackson in advance, asked their parishioners to boycott the company's products. Within a few days, the company capitulated, offering to resolve the impasse: they would add 44 jobs, or 20 percent of their job force, for black ghetto residents.

"Our tactics are not ones of terror," Jackson asserted. "Our biggest concern is to develop a relationship so that the company has a respect for the consumer and the consumer will have respect for the company." As buying power increases for members of the black community, he said, "they will be able to spend more money. So it benefits both sides."[3]

Describing the essential purpose of Operation Breadbasket, Jackson said that blacks must be able to control the basic resources of the communities in which they lived. "We want to control the banks, the trades, the building construction and the education of our children. This desire on our part is a defensive strategy evolved in order to stop whites from controlling our community and removing the profits and income that belong to black people. Our programs are dictated by the private-enterprise economy in which we find ourselves."[4]

Under Jackson's guidance, Operation Breadbasket repeated its first success with others. Jackson's image increasingly began to appear in Chicago newspapers. He seemed always to be in motion, giving impromptu lectures about black pride, organizing meetings with assorted ministers, businessmen, and politicians around town, and forcefully and uniquely inserting himself in the life of the city. He was determined that no light would shine brighter than his own.

More than six feet tall with jet-black hair, a mustache, and olive-colored skin, he often wore dashikis (African-style shirts). He was a striking figure. Elegantly dangerous he seemed to some, a radical who somehow had made a place for himself among the business suits of the city.

Richard Hatcher, a longtime associate of Jackson at Operation Breadbasket and later mayor of Indianapolis, remembered meeting Jackson for the first time at an organizational meeting in an old theater building that had no heat. "It had to be 10 degrees outside. He had called this meeting to organize Breadbasket and I guess the thing that sticks out in my mind was this very tall, compelling figure. We were in a circle, all holding hands—really to stay warm because there was no heat in the theater. We sang a song and then he began to speak. And it was just mesmerizing. He has this very pronounced Southern drawl and yet the kinds of things he was saying sounded very profound."[5] Jackson, said Hatcher, was the most intense man he ever met. There was little room for chatting and idling. He was always talking about issues, about next steps, his mind whirling through a tornado of ideas, always pressing others to keep moving.

KING TAKES ON CHICAGO

At the same time Jackson was launching his Operation Breadbasket campaigns in Chicago, black ghettos in a number of cities across the country were erupting in riots. As the civil rights movement directly challenged the existing economic and political power structures, as it demonstrated that reformers could indeed make a difference in the lives of ordinary minority citizens, it inevitably raised expectations and intensified pressures for immediate change. Thousands of black Americans who had been living their lives resigned to the racial caste system that deprived them of basic rights and opportunities now saw the chance for something better. However, as increasingly strident demands for change were met with fierce resistance and racial animosity, the delicate stability in many urban centers of America blew apart.

In August 1965, the Los Angeles neighborhood of Watts had exploded in riots after a traffic incident. The hostility between the black neighborhood and the Los Angeles police inflamed throughout the summer, erupted into such chaos and violence that more than 30 people were killed, almost all of them black. More than 3,500 people were arrested, many for looting stores and setting fire to buildings and automobiles. The clash was of such a magnitude that the National Guard was called out to restore order.

King was deeply distressed by the racial violence. Although he was concerned that his efforts in large northern cities might lead to heated exchanges between protestors and law enforcement and the public, he nevertheless believed that the civil rights movement must continue to mount pressure for equal treatment and economic independence. He thus prepared for Chicago.

With Jackson's help and with the assistance of other SCLC and civil rights leaders, he organized local ministers and planned for marches and boycotts. In early 1966, King and two SCLC aides rented a four-room apartment in a Chicago ghetto. King's move into the residence was a visible and personal protest in the fight for better housing and economic conditions for blacks. This was a campaign against slums, and King had put himself in the middle of one. He would fight for open housing against an entrenched social order that would fiercely resist.

On July 10, 1966, after addressing more than 50,000 people at Soldier Field, Chicago's massive football field on the shore of Lake Michigan, King led the marchers to City Hall, where he posted demands for what he called "The Non-Violent Freedom Fighters" on the door of Mayor Richard Daley. The demands sought to end discrimination in housing, employment, and schools in Chicago. Infuriated at King's invasion into his city and the challenge to his authority, Daley had refused to meet with King.

On July 12, as the toll of summer heat fueled the intensity generated by King's march, riots erupted on Chicago West Side. When police killed two black youths, Illinois governor Otto Kerner ordered 4,000 National Guardsmen to Chicago.

The demonstrations continued. On August 5, as King led another march through an area in southwestern Chicago, he and other marchers were pelted with stones by an angry crowd. King was startled at the venom and hatred that he saw from the crowds.

Over succeeding weeks, as tensions in the city over the continuing protests mounted, the mayor finally called a meeting at the Palmer House Hotel with King on August 26, 1966. The talks, in which Jackson participated, soon resulted in an open housing agreement that supposedly made it possible for blacks in Chicago to move into other areas of the city. King told the press that his ghetto busting campaign was paying dividends.

But the Palmer House agreement, as King and others would soon realize, did not have the necessary force of law or government behind it. It had no teeth. Although some progress would come from the negotiations, the agreement would be largely ignored.

In the summer of 1967, many of King's deepest worries about the growing violence in the country were realized. America's ghettos were aflame. Even as earlier victories had mounted in the civil rights campaign against segregation and disfranchisement and had raised hopes in the black communities around the country for progress toward racial equality, the attempts to force economic rights in the North met with a fiery resistance that even King had not foreseen. The sight of rioting black youths in the inner cities fighting with police became a frightening if not uncommon spectacle on American television news. More than 75 cities witnessed especially brutal confrontations in 1967 alone.

In Newark, New Jersey, 26 blacks lost their lives amid the carnage, and in Detroit, Michigan, riots lasted a full week with the city's black areas ablaze and enveloped by billowing black clouds of smoke. More than 40 individuals lost their lives in the Detroit riots. King condemned the violence, but his harshest criticism was for the social conditions that he believed led to the violence. When King had visited Watts in 1975 after the riots, he said that officials in the city should have anticipated the gathering storm about to strike the city since the unemployment rate in Watts had "soared above the depression rate" and since "population density of Watts became worst in the nation."[6]

America's war with itself over racial equality and equal rights, King knew, would be a long one.

LOAVES FROM THE BREADBASKET

After opening victories in the campaign against relatively small businesses, Jackson turned to the Atlantic & Pacific Company (A&P), one of the country's largest grocery chains. For more than six months, Breadbasket led a boycott of most of the 36 A&P stores in black areas of Chicago. With housewives and clergymen boosting the boycott with pickets in front of the various stores and with surprising discipline among the black community in staying away from the stores, Operation Breadbasket soon had another victory. So successful was the boycott that business in some of the stores dropped almost completely. Inside the stores, down aisle after aisle, the appearance was eerie, as if the stores were essentially closed.

By the time the boycott played itself out, the grocery chain promised to make available nearly 1,000 jobs. Soon, nearly 200 blacks had jobs—from delivery boys to department managers. In addition, the chain agreed to increase its sale of products produced by black businessmen, to use black-owned janitorial and exterminating companies, and to use black-owned banks as business partners in ghetto areas.

Jewel Tea Company hired more than 600 black employees after Jackson's troops turned up the heat. Dozens of other companies did not wait for the actual boycotts to begin but notified Jackson that new jobs were opening up for blacks. "You can't calculate the number of jobs made available because they hear those footsteps coming," Jackson told a reporter.[7]

The campaign also employed other tactics. It threatened boycotts against stores that did not stock goods produced by black enterprises. One of the products, Mumbo Barbecue Sauce, increased its business 600 percent within only a few months. The campaign even began to organize companies to match them with the customer base. A sanitation company, organized by Operation Breadbasket, began to service many of the A&P stores.

"I think he saw the ministry as a way of influencing events, influencing currents in the United States, and of course, the world," said Calvin Morris, one of Jackson's lieutenants in Operation Breadbasket. "Because one of the things that first struck me about Jesse when I first met him was the fact that he thought globally about himself and he saw himself in places that young Negro boys like ourselves didn't see."[8]

King lauded Jackson's work in Chicago, especially for another important initiative. Jackson's group spearheaded the development of black-controlled financial institutions that were sensitive to the problems of poverty in the black communities. As black-run banks began to deal with the larger chain organizations in Chicago and acquired greater resources, they in turn could make loans to black businessmen who could hire black workers who would then have greater financial resources of their own to spend. Operation Breadbasket was thus helping to create an economic cycle of production and consumerism within those communities.

Jackson's work in Chicago was so successful that he was asked to expand operations of Operation Breadbasket to other cities. He was named national director. From Brooklyn, New York, to Los Angeles, California, Breadbasket organized 15 infant local chapters and began attempting to copy the successes of Chicago. However, the local organizations often lacked the finances and the charismatic leaders to bring together the disparate parts that Jackson had done in Chicago—from local civil rights groups to black church members.

Self-confident and audacious, Jackson began to consider any individual only a phone call away. Entertainers, politicians, and corporate leaders—all were in Jackson's scope. He was seemingly indefatigable despite the fact that, as his friends over the years began to learn, he suffered from sickle-cell disease, a red blood cell disorder that can cause pain, low blood count, and anemia. Hospitalized several times for viruses contracted because of the disease, Jackson was placed on a strict regimen of medicine. Despite his fragile health, he continued at a frantic pace.

Jackson began to schedule Saturday morning rallies of Operation Breadbasket for the public. Although the crowds increasingly got larger and the locations changed from storefronts to movie theaters, the programs and the messages remained similar, and Jackson made every effort he possibly could to attend.

The first hour rocked with the sounds of gospel music with an orchestra and choir. Around the location were tables displaying products manufactured by black entrepreneurs and messages to use the services of black-run businesses. Jackson's own words were sermonlike, interspersed with quotations from the Bible, street slang, rhymes, and quotations from theologians, writers, and biblical scribes. As Jackson's rhythm and beat swelled, so did the sounds from the crowd, as in a black church. He sought audience reaction: "Am I speaking the truth?" or "Are you with me?" The responses reverberated throughout the crowd: "Tell them, Reverend!" "Amen!" and "Right on!" and sounds from the piano and organ highlighted the message. Sometimes he stopped in the middle of the sermon to ask a soloist to sing a particular hymn. Other times, he rolled to the conclusion, perspiration dripping from his forehead, the pace now frantic and imploring, calling the audience to come together for each other, to rally for all those in need, to join in following the salient teachings of the gospel—to feed and clothe the poor and hungry. After the meeting, the orchestra and singers joined in a version of the civil rights marching song "We Shall Overcome," and the audience, swaying with the music and exuberantly joining in the singing, held hands.

A DIVERSION TO MEMPHIS

On December 4, 1967, in Atlanta, Martin Luther King held a press conference announcing that the SCLC "will lead waves of the nation's poor and disinherited to Washington, D.C. next spring to demand redress of their grievances by the U.S. government and to secure at least jobs or income for all. We will go there, we will demand to be heard, and we will stay until America responds. If this means forcible repression of our movement we will confront it, for we have done this before. If this means scorn or ridicule we embrace it, for that is what America's poor now receive."[9]

Instead of scaling back his efforts to fight poverty in the face of overwhelming resistance, King announced that he would lead this nonviolent march to petition the U.S. government for specific reforms. From cities and counties around the country, SCLC members would gather in separate groups and make their way to Washington.

Unlike the 1963 March on Washington that had culminated with King's historic speech at the Lincoln Memorial, this would not be a one-day affair, King explained. The marchers would not leave Washington but would stay until some government action was taken to alleviate poverty and unemployment. It took a Selma, King said, before the government moved to affirm the fundamental right of voting to black Americans; it took a Birmingham before the government moved to ensure the right of all Americans to public accommodations. His call was not just for black Americans, he said, but to all of America's poor—whites, Indians, Mexican Americans, Puerto Ricans, and others. The marchers would come to Washington, he said, to channel into constructive action the frustration and rage that had ignited the cities in riots, to compel the government to come to the aid of those suffering economic deprivation and discrimination. The marchers would seek a $12 billion "Economic Bill of Rights" guaranteeing employment to the able-bodied, incomes to those unable to work, and an end to housing discrimination.

A number of King's lieutenants, including Jackson and Andrew Young, were not enthusiastic about the idea of the Poor People's Campaign. King told his associates that he expected a hostile reception in Washington. Like Mayor Richard Daley of Chicago, President Lyndon B. Johnson, King realized, would react coldly to the notion that demonstrators would come to the seat of the national government, engage in overt civil protests, and expect the government to yield to their demands.

King not only realized that jail was a distinct possibility but actually warned Jackson and others that their participation might mean a prison sentence. King had decided to escalate the struggle and was willing to pay a price. Although many of them had doubts, King finally persuaded Jackson and the others to join the effort despite his gloomy predictions.

At a meeting in Atlanta, Jackson and others realized the depths of despair that was now plaguing King. The nationwide riots, the experience in Chicago, and the continuing escalation of the Vietnam War—the increasingly unpopular effort of the United States to stop communism in Southeast Asia, which King had begun to denounce—all this bore down on the civil rights leader like a great weight. The only response to the troubles that had befallen the country, King told his friends, was to carry on with the work, to fight even harder, and to rally together and convince the nation's leadership to follow a course toward justice.

As King's plans for the Poor People's Campaign proceeded, another labor fight involving black workers came to his attention. In Memphis, Tennessee, black sanitation workers had banded together in a strike against the city. They had formed a union and, carrying signs with the words "I Am a Man," lobbied for better working conditions and pay. Newly elected mayor Harry Loebe refused to deal with strike leaders and threatened to fire every striker if they failed to return to work. In early February, when only about one-fourth of the city's sanitation trucks were at work, the city began to hire scab labor.

When community civil rights groups and labor leaders contacted the King organization asking for support, King considered intervening. Although a number of his aides feared that a trip to Memphis would seriously interrupt plans for the Poor People's March, King felt that he could not turn his back on the poorest of workers in Memphis.

On March 28, King, flanked by nearly 200 preachers, was once again on the streets in a major American city leading a protest on behalf of economic and racial justice. The marchers were met with police mace, tear gas, and gunfire. A 16-year-old boy was shot. Nearly 300 marchers were rounded up and jailed, most for breaking windows and some for looting stores. About 60 injuries were reported. National Guardsmen moved into the city. Memphis was in a state of siege.

King, along with other leaders of the SCLC, decided to remain for a few days longer in Memphis to work with city leaders and strikers in an effort to resolve the crisis. They had checked into an inexpensive, small, two-story motel just outside the downtown area. Originally, in the 1920s, it was named the Windsor, and it was one of the only hotels in downtown Atlanta that housed blacks. It was now called the Lorraine.

NOTES

1. Frontline, "Interview with Dr. Calvin Morris," http://www.pbs.org/wgbh/pages/frontline/jesse/interviews/morris.html.

2. Michael Eric Dyson, *I May Not Get There with You: The True Martin Luther King, Jr.* (New York: Touchstone, 2000), 81–82.

3. "Black Pocketbook Power," *Time*, March 1, 1968, 17.

4. "Jesse Jackson: A Candid Conversation with the Fiery Heir Apparent to Martin Luther King," *Playboy*, November 1969, http://www.geocities.com/heartland/9766/jackson.htm.

5. Frontline, "Interview with Richard Hatcher," http://www.pbs.org/wgbh/pages/frontline/jesse/interviews/hatcher.html.

6. Dyson, *I May Not Get There with You*, 85.

7. "Black Pocketbook Power."

8. Frontline, "Interview with Dr. Calvin Morris," http://www.pbs.org/wgbh/pages/frontline/jesse/interviews/morris.html.

9. "Press Conference Announcing the Poor People's Campaign," December 4, 1967, Atlanta, Georgia, http://www.stanford.edu/group/King/publications/papers/unpub/671204-003_Announcing_Poor_Peoples_campaign.htm.

Chapter 6

ASSASSINATION AND AFTERMATH

On the evening of April 3, 1968, Martin Luther King Jr., facing an injunction by Memphis city officials preventing him from leading another march in behalf of striking sanitation workers, delivered a speech at the Mason Temple. Inspiring, pensive, and defiant, King talked about how far those people surrounding him had together come in the movement, how overwhelming had been the struggle, and how daunting remained the challenges ahead. He talked about a recent incident in which a troubled black woman had knifed him and that the knife had come perilously close to his aorta. He talked about the uncertainty of his own future and about recent threats on his own life. He told them to hold together for the cause of social equality no matter what happened.

In the middle of the speech, he talked about Operation Breadbasket and the efforts of the SCLC to force American society to accept black businesses and black consumers as equals.

> We are asking you tonight, to go out and tell your neighbors not to buy Coca-Cola in Memphis. Go by and tell them not to buy Sealtest milk. Tell them not to buy—what is the other bread?—Wonder Bread. And what is the other bread company, Jesse? Tell them not to buy Hart's bread. As Jesse Jackson has said, up to now, only the garbage men have been feeling pain; now we must kind of redistribute the pain. We are choosing these companies because they haven't been fair in their hiring policies; and we are choosing them because they can begin the

process of saying they are going to support the needs and the rights of these men who are on strike.[1]

Jesse Jackson would look on those words as his last assignment from King.

Then, in a remarkably prescient moment, King looked forward to difficult days ahead: "But it doesn't matter with me now. Because I've been to the mountaintop. And I don't mind. Like anybody, I would like to live a long life. Longevity has its place. But I'm not concerned about that now. I just want to do God's will. And He's allowed me to go up to the mountain. And I've looked over. And I've seen the promised land. I may not get there with you. But I want you to know tonight, that we, as a people, will get will get to the promised land. And I'm happy, tonight. I'm not worried about anything. I'm not fearing any man. Mine eyes have seen the glory of the coming of the Lord."[2]

Early the following morning, April 4, 1968, the SCLC had good news for King and his associates. The injunction against the march had been lifted. At midday, preparing to leave the Lorraine Motel to meet with march organizers, King stepped out from his room on the second floor. Jackson, from the parking lot below, and King exchanged a few remarks, and Jackson introduced Ben Branch, a musician and singer from the Operation Breadbasket orchestra in Chicago. King called out to Branch that he hoped Branch could sing "Precious Lord."

Then they all heard the crack of the rifle shot. As King, hit in the face and neck, crumpled on the balcony floor, Jackson and others raced to his side. Ralph Abernathy, his closest friend, cradled him. Blood covered the balcony. Jesse wiped some of it on his shirt.

Reverend Samuel Kyles was also there. Pastor of the Monumental Baptist Church in Memphis and longtime civil rights activist, Kyles was with King and Abernathy in a room of the Lorraine for the last hour of King's life. Kyles had helped arrange for the upcoming march and had been working on the sanitation workers' strike since the beginning. That evening, King was to have had dinner at Kyle's home, along with Jackson.

"About a quarter of 6:00 we walked out onto the balcony," Kyles remembered. He was greeting people he had not seen. Somebody said, 'It's going to be cold Doc, get your coat.' He didn't go back in the room. He went to the door and said, 'Ralph, get my coat.' Ralph was in the room putting on shaving lotion. Ralph said, 'I'll get your coat.' He went back to the railing of the balcony and was greeting people again. He said something to Jesse Jackson and said something to some other people. We stood together. I said, 'Come on, guys. Let's go.'"

Since that day, Kyles has reflected on why he happened to be at that place at that time. He concluded that he was there to be a witness. "Martin Luther King, Jr. didn't die in some foolish, untoward way. He didn't overdose. He wasn't shot by a jealous lover. He died helping garbage workers."[3]

Kyles also pointed out, as did others, that King had mentioned on occasion that he might never reach age 40. When the bullet ended his life that day in Memphis, he was 39.

As other leaders of the SCLC and friends of King stayed for a few days in Memphis preparing for King's funeral and making other immediate arrangements for the Poor People's Campaign, Jackson, still wearing the turtleneck shirt stained with the blood of King, left for Chicago. When Jackie picked him up at the Chicago airport, the two barely spoke on their way home. For days, Jackie remembered, Jessie kept the shirt on, night and day. Despite mutual agreement with the SCLC leadership that no contact be made with the press until Mrs. Coretta King had a chance to communicate her own thoughts and wishes, Jesse made other plans. He would make his own personal testimony about what happened in Memphis.

Jackie Jackson remembered Jesse continuing to wear the shirt: "About three days, four days, five days to a week. I know it was a long time to walk around in the same clothing. And he just didn't have the ability to move beyond it. And it was very painful for him and for me also. Because the assassination in Memphis, we physically lost one individual. But actually, we lost many lives there. And a portion of my husband's life and many of the members of SCLC remained on that balcony in Memphis." Gradually, as the depression and shock wore thinner, Jackson readied himself to move on.[4]

The following morning Jackson appeared on the *Today* show. Later that day, he went to the Chicago City Council's memorial service for King, asked Mayor Daley to speak, and called for an end of rioting that had begun in Chicago and other cities around the country. Dramatically pointing to his shirt, Jackson declared that King's blood was shed for the rights of the poor and his vision for racial reconciliation. "This blood is on the chest and hands of those who would not have welcomed him here yesterday," Jackson exclaimed. A fitting memorial to the slain civil rights leader, he said, "would not be to sit here looking sad and pious ... but to behave differently."[5]

Jackson's behavior in Chicago outraged many of his associates in the SCLC and angered King's widow. They saw Jessie as an unabashed opportunist whose allegiance at this critical time in the long movement for civil rights was not to the cause but to himself. Even for some of Jackson's most ardent supporters, his behavior in this instance was contemptuous. Civil rights leader and then university professor Roger Wilkins later remarked that going on television with a blood-soaked shirt was something he would not have done. "But on the other hand, given Jesse's sense of drama and emotionalism…you know, anybody who's ever been through a family funeral knows that people do things around the time of the death that later they wish they hadn't done."[6]

But almost all of King's associates believed that Jackson had gone much too far—that he was stroking fires of self-promotion and leading on the media, which were already primed to anoint Jackson the next great black leader. Jackson had opened a great rift between himself and a number of other SCLC leaders that would never mend.

Although genuinely grieved by the death of King to the point of despair, Jackson had done what he had always done: he seized an opportunity. Jackson's friend Calvin Morris later said, "Tibby, his grandmother's right, Jesse always senses the moment. And it was an epochical moment. And he was there. And he responded, some would say used it, but I would say he responded to the moment so that it wasn't time for a whole lot of grief. There was still work to be done, there was still explanations to be made, there were still arrangements to be done, etc. and so forth."[7]

As news of King's assassination swept the nation and the world, racial violence flared in more than 100 cities across the United States. Militant black leaders such as Stokely Carmichael, who had preached a more aggressive fight for black rights than King, now called for harsh retaliation against the white power structure. President Johnson, expressing sorrow and outrage for the assassination, called for restraint. Nevertheless, Johnson, fearing widespread violence, was forced to dispatch military troops and National Guard units to a number of cities.

On April 8, Reverend Ralph Abernathy, the successor to King as president of the SCLC, led more than 40,000 marchers in Memphis to honor King and to show continuing support for the sanitation workers. Within eight days, the city and the workers had reached a settlement.

On April 9, mourners gathered at Ebenezer Baptist Church in Atlanta, where King had served as copastor. The nation's political and social elite, from Jacqueline Kennedy to Supreme Court Justice Thurgood Marshall, attended. Outside the church, along Auburn Street, thousands gathered. Later, King's coffin, pulled on a cart by two mules, rolled through Atlanta's streets to Southview Cemetery.

Two months later, following an international manhunt, a white seg-regationist loner and small-time criminal named James Earl Ray was arrested in London for King's assassination. Ray was extradited to the United States, and Tennessee prosecutors agreed in a plea bargain not to seek the death penalty if Ray pled guilty to murder charges. Many questions later swirled around the case as Ray first confessed and then recanted the crime. Was he the killer? Did he have accomplices? Over the years, the King family came to believe that someone other than Ray had actually committed the crime. Jackson definitely believed that Ray was part of a larger conspiracy to kill King.

Whatever the entire truth of the King assassination, Jackson said later of the man he revered that "it was Dr. King who crossed the frontier, who made a permanent break with the past. I grew up in the period from 1955 to 1965, and that time was dominated by his courage and strength, as opposed to the previous mass docility of black men. Dr. King was a surprise for a lot of whites who had conned themselves into believing that Negroes were really inferior. He was intelligent, moral, eloquent and courageous."[8]

RESURRECTION CITY

When Martin Luther King Jr. had conceived of the idea of the Poor People's Campaign, he had placed the SCLC in a new and difficult position outside its usual role of fighting for the civil rights for black Americans. This would be a campaign to challenge the government to intervene in an issue that was beyond legal rights, beyond the rights of blacks, and beyond the scope of anything the SCLC had ever attempted. Demanding economic relief for America's impoverished, regardless of racial background, the campaign sought to employ King's usual tactics of nonviolent confrontation. But the effort played out against a national backdrop of escalating violence and contention. The rise of militant black nationalist groups and their leaders who saw the nonviolent tactics of King and his organization outdated and ineffectual; the deepening havoc of the Vietnam War and the increasing militancy of those opposed to it; and the assassination of King and then of Robert F. Kennedy, whose presidential campaign in 1968 was centered on his opposition to the war and support for the poor—in the midst of all of this national turmoil, the Poor People's Campaign began. Its specific aim was a $30 billion antipoverty package that included a commitment to full employment, a guaranteed annual income, and increased construction of low-income housing.

On May 2, under a blistering sun, led by a mule-drawn wagon, and with more than 1,000 marchers singing and chanting, the campaign started, appropriately, from the Lorraine Motel. They walked to the poorest section of Memphis, where 300 individuals boarded buses for Marks, Mississippi. Picking up additional protestors at other towns and cities along the way, they headed to Washington.

From different locations around the United States, including Boston, Chicago, Denver, and Los Angeles, protestors boarded buses, cars, and trains. They carried various distinctive names—the "Appalachia Trail," the "Freedom Train," and the "Indian Trail." Finally, in mid-May, the "Eastern Caravan," with some 800 people, including 200 Puerto Ricans from New York City, reached the nation's capital.

The campaign brought nearly 3,000 people to Washington, D.C., to live for almost six weeks. They included a mix of races and cultures, and their professions ranged from factory worker to sharecropper to single mother. Their residence was in one of the most revered settings in the United States, flanking the reflecting pool on the Washington Mall in the shadow of the Lincoln Memorial. It was called "Resurrection City, USA," and for the short time of its existence, it had its own ZIP code—20013.

The camp also had its own doctors, dentists, a dining hall, and a nursery, all donated from various charitable enterprises. And it had its own mayor—Jesse Jackson. In his work at Operation Breadbasket in Chicago, Jackson had begun to work closely with street gang members and others on society's fringes not only as encouragement to give up violence as a way of life but also to enlist their help in reaching others in the poor sections of Chicago. Jackson was learning to speak the language of the street as well as the language of the black churches and the political language of the soapbox. Thus, he was a perfect choice to attempt to achieve something positive from this strange shantytown protest anchored in the heart of Washington.

But if the setting was one of grandeur, the conditions, nevertheless, became nearly unbearable. For 28 of the 42 days of the duration of the Poor People's Campaign, driving rains turned the grassy parkland into a swamp. With the pelting downpours and the constant tramping by the people who began to take up residence in the temporary plywood shacks and tents, the ground became a shifting, rolling sink of mud into which feet, ankles, and, in some cases, legs would suddenly plunge. Nevertheless, the protestors, with varying degrees of enthusiasm, set up personal living quarters and decorated the shacks with graffiti designations, from "OOO Poor Avenue" to "Soul House No. 1 1/2." They earned no wages while at the city, and many left within the first two weeks. Others held on despite the rain and the unusually chilly May and June nights. With huge oil drums burning the trash from Resurrection City, the nights around the Lincoln Memorial took on an eerie cast.

March organizers led groups of protestors to various locations in Washington, met with public officials, tried to get as much airtime on radio and television as possible, and attempted to extract whatever promises of help from the federal government as they could in the fight to alleviate poverty. With his characteristic energy and imagination, Jackson, especially, continued to search for ways to get attention for the campaign. "We have been the nation's laborers, her waiters. Our women have raised her Presidents on their knees. We have made cotton king. We have built the highways. We have died in wartime fighting.... America worked us for 350 years without paying us. Now we deserve a job or an income."[9]

To a group of lawmakers holding a hearing in a third-floor room of the U.S. House of Representatives Rayburn Building on Capitol Hill, the sound from below, in its sermon cadences, came through. The voice was that of Jesse Jackson using a bullhorn, leading a group of demonstrators seeking jobs and greater income for the nation's poor. After a conference between congressional leaders and the police, Jackson and about 300 of his followers were allowed to enter the building and make their case directly. For more than an hour, Jackson held forth, assisted by a few songs from the group and a prayer. Jackson was leading an impromptu revival. He said to God, "We have been told 'no' too often, when the answer should have been 'yes.'" From the group came the response, "Oh, yes, Lord!" The meeting lasted more than an hour. Although Jackson achieved rapt attention from the members of Congress, he received no promises of reform.[10]

At one point in the campaign, Jackson conceived the notion of escorting many of the people in Resurrection City to government cafeterias and then demanding that they be fed at the expense of the government. The government officials acquiesced. These small triumphs were few. If the object had been to use Resurrection City as a symbol of protest to spread the message of the campaign, the chaos and disappointment that soon fell along with the rain threatened to sink the entire enterprise.

Civil rights leader Roger Wilkins remembered Jackson plunging into a crowd in the black section of Washington amidst the anger and confusion and a spirit of anarchy in the air and "preaching the riot out of a crowd." It occurred at 14th and U Streets, a bustling section in the black community. A crowd of angry demonstrators, encouraged by the incendiary rhetoric of militants, had ominously formed, and the air was thick with threats of violence. Into the mix stepped Jackson. Known in the black community as a follower of King and his nonviolent teachings, Jackson, nevertheless, from the back of a flatbed truck, demonstrated his remarkable ability to soften tough situations. He talked them down, told them they mattered, and made sense to them in a language they could understand. Wilkins remembered hearing Jackson use a kind of rap response with the refrain "I Am Somebody" that he had heard used by King. Tearing down the neighborhoods, Jackson insisted, was not the answer to their problems. They were somebody, and they must fight for their rights, he preached, but not with firebombs or handguns. "He was willing to risk rejection by this crowd," Wilkins said, "because he knew that a riot would undercut the whole moral authority of the Poor People's Campaign and also the moral authority of the poor people who were gathered there. And he did it. He did."[11]

As the public and the press began to focus on the increasingly deplorable physical conditions of Resurrection City, the question for the city and Congress became less about the issues of poverty and more about cleaning up the mess and returning the city to its normal conditions. Some of the campaign's organizers began to point out that some of the homes left behind by the campaign's poor across the country were no better than the shacks in the mud of Resurrection City. Calvin Trillin, political pundit and humorist and supporter of the aims of the movement, wrote, "The poor in Resurrection City have come to Washington to show that the poor in America are sick, dirty, disorganized, and powerless—and they are criticized daily for being sick, dirty, disorganized, and powerless."[12]

Nevertheless, by the end of June, even some of the campaign's most ardent supporters were urging the leaders to end the protest. Representative Robert Nix, a black congressman from Philadelphia, urged campaign leader Abernathy to disband the group and leave a small task force behind to continue lobbying efforts. Among his fellow members of Congress, he said, there was "no enthusiasm" for the Poor People's Campaign.[13]

On June 19, 1968, the campaign culminated with a "Solidarity Day" march that included not only the campaign organizers and the remaining residents of the shantytown but also thousands of other Americans who turned out to show support for the aims of the Poor People's Campaign. Along with other speakers, Jackson stood at what by now seemed to him a personal shrine—the Lincoln Memorial—where five years earlier he had been among the many thousands who had gathered at the March on

Washington to hear his mentor, Martin Luther King Jr., give the legendary "I Have a Dream" speech.

Jackson declared, "Whereas we stand in the shadows of Lincoln the Emancipator who freed us into capitalism without capital. Whereas we stand in a land of surplus food with 10 million starving citizens, and whereas the soil bank has become Holy Land…the land on which some men swim in wealth while others drown in tears from broken promises, destroyed dreams and blasted hopes.… For the life we live and the life we love we vow to fight for a new sensitive and sensible economic order in that all men need a job or an income if they are to have human dignity; all men deserve a job or an income for it is not alone by men's work but by God's grace that America is so fertile and rich."[14]

Resurrection City, USA, finally closed down on the morning of June 24 at the hands of nearly 1,000 policemen. Some of the demonstrators did not go peacefully. As the crowds began to appear threatening, the police used more than 1,000 tear gas grenades to clear out the area on the Mall. They arrested 175 people, including Reverend Abernathy.

Jackson had not been enthusiastic about the Poor People's Campaign from its inception. He had feared that its tactics and strategic approach, even with Martin Luther King Jr. involved, were likely doomed to produce contention and annoyance rather than real economic reform. He had been right. Nevertheless, his energies in Washington during the several weeks of the protest never flagged and he began to see much merit in the original idea. He was fully behind the ultimate goals that King had laid out—the fight to unite working-class people of all races and the commitment to eradicate poverty in a land of plenty. It was this kind of militant economic populism, fighting for the rights of the underclasses against the power and concentration of wealth and big business, that was behind Operation Breadbasket. It was this fight that he would now take to greater levels.

NOTES

1. "I've Been to the Mountaintop," speech delivered April 3, 1968, Memphis, Tennessee, http://www.americanrhetoric.com/speeches/mlkivebeentothemountaintop.htm.

2. "I've Been to the Mountaintop."

3. "On the Balcony with Dr. King," http://www.explorefaith.org/reflections52.htm.

4. Frontline, "Interview: Jackie Jackson," http://www.pbs.org/wgbh/pages/frontline/jesse/interviews/jackie.html.

5. *New York Times*, July 9, 1972.

6. Marshall Frady, *Jesse: The Life and Pilgrimage of Jesse Jackson* (New York: Random House, 1996), 233.

7. Frontline, "Interview with Dr. Calvin Morris," http://www.pbs.org/wgbh/pages/frontline/jesse/interviews/morris.html.

8. "Jesse Jackson: A Candid Conversation with the Fiery Heir Apparent to Martin Luther King," *Playboy*, November 1969, http://www.geocities.com/heartland/9766/jackson.htm.

9. *New York Times*, May 24, 1968.

10. *Washington Post*, May 26, 1968.

11. Frontline, "Interview with Roger Wilkins," http://www.pbs.org/wgbh/pages/frontline/jesse/interviews/wilkins.html.

12. Calvin Trillin, "U.S. Journal: Resurrection City," *The New Yorker*, June 15, 1968, 71.

13. *New York Times*, June 30, 1968.

14. Robert T. Chase, "Class Resurrection: The Poor People's Campaign of 1968 and Resurrection City," George Mason University, http://etext.lib.virginia.edu/journals/EH/EH40/chase40.html.

What Jesse Jackson faced in his youth—boy at a drinking fountain at the county courthouse, Halifax, North Carolina, 1940s. Courtesy of the Library of Congress, LC-USF3301-001112-M1.

Bus station, Durham, North Carolina, 1940. Courtesy of the Library of Congress, Farm Security Administration, Office of War Information Photograph Collection.

Crowds in front of the Lincoln Memorial for the March on Washington, 1963. Courtesy of the Library of Congress, LC-U0-10371-27A.

Jesse Jackson speaks at the annual convention of Operation Push, July 1973. Photo from the National Archives and Records Administration, Still Picture Records, ARC Identifier 556252.

Jackson at March for Jobs at the White House, January 1975. Courtesy of the Library of Congress, LC-U9-30656B-10.

Jesse Jackson, 1983. Courtesy of the Library of Congress, LC-U9-41583-29.

Jackson announcing his candidacy for President, Washington, D.C., 1984. Photo from the National Archives and Records Administration, Still Picture Records, RG306, PSE, 83-3573.

Chapter 7

OPERATION PUSH

BREAKING AWAY

Saturday mornings on Chicago's South Side could rock. Want to hear some great jazz and rhythm and blues, some lively and inspiring preaching, and even some animated discussions of current events? Go over to Operation Breadbasket's headquarters and take in the scene. On one October Saturday morning in 1969, you could see the fabulous alto saxophonist Cannonball Adderley, with his younger brother Nat on the cornet, and bask in the exuberant sounds of what became known as "soul jazz."

As Reverend Jesse Jackson appears on stage to open the proceedings, chants of "Jesse" echo throughout the room. In front of a portrait of Martin Luther King Jr., he stands before the group clutching the lectern, then pumps his fist, jabs the air, and whips into a brief speech on standing up for human rights and fighting to make a difference for black Americans in a white man's world. His staccato sentences rising in intensity, and the crowd cheers.

Adderley's Quintet then launches into the musical performances with "Walk Tall," a number written by keyboardist Joe Zawinul in honor of Jackson, a piece perfectly fitting for the message of the day—that poor peoples must unite to make meaningful change. The quintet also plays another piece written by Zawinul called "Country Preacher," a term that Jackson sometimes uses in referring to his own down-to-earth oratory.

On this day, however, the spotlight is on the magical sax of the Cannonball, a former high school band director in Florida who has become one of the nation's most popular jazzmen. Adderley does some preaching on his own during the performance, and the audience shouts approval with every exhortation and cue.

Community power—this is what Jackson wants to cultivate; this is the energy he wants to tap. With each "Amen" and each "Tell it like it is," his emotions soar. This is something akin to a raucous Baptist church meeting back in Greenville, South Carolina, and Jackson is in his element. Through the music and the hand clapping, the singing, and the spontaneous shouts of the crowd, he and they are on a roll now.

Not only did Jackson turn the Operation Breadbasket headquarters into a kind of community center, but his own home in these years also became a central meeting place. Jackie later looked back to the years after Martin Luther King's assassination as a critical transition period for both Jackson and herself. They tried in Chicago, she later remembered, to establish within the community the kind of close personal relationships and togetherness they had known in the South during the momentous times of civil rights protest.

Through Jackson's ability to inspire mutual cooperation and dedication to the cause, Operation Breadbasket became a formidable social and political organization. Although it technically was still a part of the SCLC, Operation Breadbasket was stamped with the giant imprint of Jackson's own dynamic personality and his own signature, a kind of social justice revival movement.

He inaugurated "Black Christmas," a celebration during Christmas week of black pride and black entrepreneurship. The festivities included a parade, replete with floats, beauty queens, and marching bands; a festival featuring products made by black-operated companies; and even a new Christmas character—Black Soul Saint—who, according to his creator, Jackson, came from the South Pole rather than the North Pole and wore African clothes adorned with the colors of the flag of the African country Ghana. Jackson's idea was yet another of his determined efforts to instill in the black community a sense of success rather than failure, hope rather than despair, and togetherness rather than division.

In the spring of 1970, influenced by the ideas behind Martin Luther King Jr.'s Poor People's Campaign, Jackson launched an initiative in Chicago called the "Illinois Hunger Campaign." Like the 1968 gathering in Washington of a diverse group of marchers composed of people from many backgrounds—from Appalachian whites to Puerto Ricans and Native Americans—Jackson organized a coalition from various poor communities in Chicago and around the state to seek help for the hungry.

"Hunger," he said, "is the one issue today that can unite people without arousing racial antagonisms."[1]

Forming several caravans, the protestors marched from various locations in Illinois to Springfield, the state capital, and held large demonstrations. Jackson made an impassioned speech from the steps of the capitol building. The message, as it had been at the foot of the Lincoln Memorial and next to Resurrection City in the March on Washington, was that hunger knew no ethnic or color bounds; hunger was indiscriminate. In a prosperous land, there must be a commitment to feed those in need, from the black ghettos of Chicago's South Side to immigrant Latino and Native American communities.

Impressed by the size of the demonstration and the fact that Jackson had melded an ethnically and culturally mixed group, the state legislature scrapped plans to cut the welfare budget in Illinois, an action that other large states, such as New York and California, were already taking to balance budget deficits. Jackson's campaign also won a bill from the legislature to provide school lunches for needy children.

Jackson's success in the Illinois Hunger Campaign demonstrated versatility, organizing acumen, and leadership skills that were astonishing given the fact that he was a relative newcomer to Chicago and the state of Illinois. He did not rest after that success; indeed, he barely hesitated.

From the wellsprings of Jackson's imagination and energy, Operation Breadbasket launched another initiative—Black Expo. For a week, at Chicago's International Amphitheater, hundreds of thousands of visitors filed past exhibits of products from black-run organizations, from dairy products and barbecue sauce to hospital equipment. They listened to political figures and celebrities discuss everything from housing and social services to political strategy. They admired paintings and other works of black artists. At one workshop, they could hear Richard Hatcher, mayor of Gary, Indiana, speak about black entrepreneurship; at another, they could hear the one-liners of comedian Bill Cosby or the vocals of singer Roberta Flack. From the Jackson Five to B. B. King, they all answered Jesse's call. He even convinced Sears Roebuck and Company to sponsor an exhibit on black inventors. Each of the yearly Black Expos featured themes such as "From Chains to Change" and "Rhythm Ain't All We Got."

By the time of the third Black Expo in 1971, the event was so hyped in the Chicago newspapers and other media that Mayor Richard Daley, no friend of the upstart Jackson and his Operation Breadbasket, showed up to share with him the lights of photographers. With attendance figures approaching 800,000, the mayor, in his political wisdom, had found it worthwhile to declare a "Black Expo Week" on behalf of the City of Chicago. The mayor smiled, Jackson smiled, but both knew that this was a major concession by Daley to Jackson's growing popularity and influence.

As Jackson's efforts in Chicago became glittering media successes, the officials of the SCLC in Atlanta became increasingly alienated from Jesse and his operation. The feeling was mutual. Jackson saw the SCLC without Martin Luther King Jr. as sorely lacking leadership and new ideas. The SCLC head, Ralph Abernathy, and others in the SCLC, most still angry with Jackson for what they regarded as grandstanding behavior immediately following the death of King, had resisted Jesse's attempts to assume a higher position in the organization. The mutual antagonisms reached a head in 1971.

SCLC leaders discovered that Jackson had incorporated the Black Expo event in his own name and those of his Chicago sponsors, not that of the SCLC, even though Operation Breadbasket was still part of the SCLC organizational structure. Although SCLC did not uncover any financial improprieties from Black Expo, the leadership suspended Jackson from the SCLC as punishment for acting outside its organization.

Beset by anger and humiliation, Jackson decided to resign. Although pained to leave the organization of King, whom he had revered, the organization under whose banner he had launched his career, Jackson decided to free himself from the constraints of his SCLC superiors and strike out on his own.

In Jackson style, he left the SCLC with much fanfare and with a major announcement: he was starting a new organization. At a gala banquet in New York's Commodore Hotel, Jackson, only 28 years old, gathered around him a team of backers with well-known names and connections, including musician Quincy Jones and Manhattan borough president Percy Sutton. Although friends said later that Jackson was anxious and worried about the break with the SCLC and somewhat uncertain about the success of his new venture, it did not outwardly show. His enthusiasm was infectious.

On December 17, 1971, he wrote a letter of resignation to the SCLC. He declared, "As we go on separate roads, I pray that our goals will remain united. We must feed the hungry, clothe the naked, and set the captive free." He signed it "Jesse Louis Jackson, The Country Preacher." He knew and they knew that Jackson was anything but a country preacher.[2]

And then, on Christmas morning 1971, in a broken-down South Side theater with no heat, Jackson announced, with almost painful symbolism, "A new child is born." He meant his organization. It was to be called People United to Serve Humanity (PUSH). It would be a national organization that would carry on many of the themes and tactics of Chicago's Operation Breadbasket, especially that of economic empowerment. It would forge a coalition, a "rainbow coalition," of blacks and whites to fight for a greater share of the country's economic and political power.

CREATING HIS OWN ACRONYM

The world of business, professional organizations, and government at all levels is littered with acronyms. In the world of civil rights, for example, everyone knew what the letters NAACP and SCLC stood for. Jackson now had his own organization with its own acronym. Unlike most of the others but characteristic of Jackson's own flair, you could pronounce it: PUSH. The acronym described not only something of its mission but also a principal characteristic of its leader.

In launching PUSH, Jackson raided Operation Breadbasket, taking with him many of his former staff and a large number of board members. His abandonment of the SCLC left that organization without its most dynamic personality.

The basic aim of PUSH, as it had been for Operation Breadbasket, was to secure jobs and food for those in need, encourage black businesses, and instill a sense of pride and identity among downtrodden minorities. In fact, however, the organization ran mostly from the instincts and inspirations of its founder. At any time, day or night, Jackson might come up with an idea. Within minutes, he would be on the phone with friends and fellow activists swapping ideas, making plans, and soliciting support, financial and otherwise. Eclectic and frantic, the organization swirled with activity, much of it nearly spontaneous and often chaotic.

He attracted many loyal workers to his side but demanded more than many were able to give. He expected everyone around him to set the same kind of frenetic pace he laid out for himself, engines running at full bore. He could be rude and domineering, ruling over the organization like a pianist over a keyboard. Often, he punched the keys much too hard. Willie Barrow, one of Jackson's closest lieutenants, once remarked that Jackson delegated most everything and expected immediate results. "All he wants to do is articulate what the situation is and lead it, but his team has to put it together. If he sees it, you ought to be able to catch it, and move it and make it happen. Grow it. If you can't, Jesse can't deal with you."[3]

Although the finances of PUSH drove several accountants dizzy, Jackson was convinced that as a servant of the people, both he and his organization would be compensated. "Now, if I'm helping you just to help me, it's not the real thing, it won't work 'cause something's missing, spiritually the whole business drops to a lower octave, understand what I'm sayin'. But real service...you cast that bread upon the waters, it'll return to you, toasted. With butter on it."[4]

Jackson was right. Rich friends and admirers such as George Jones, head of the Joe Louis Milk Company, and Hugh Hefner, founder of *Playboy* magazine, made sure not only that Jackson and his associates made the payroll but also that they prospered. It would not be too long until the toasted bread with butter included a Lincoln Continental, a 15-room Tudor-style house with some stained-glass windows on a tree-lined boulevard that once housed Chicago's business squires, and even financial help to pay for his children's school tuition. The Jackson family would live in style; it would be far from Haynie Street in Greenville, South Carolina. Soon, the Jacksons would enjoy free landscaping services and would dine in elegant restaurants. The reverend could choose from his closet a number of pin-striped Brooks Brothers suits for certain occasions and African-styled threads for others.

From the time of their marriage on the last day of December 1962, Jesse and Jackie had five children. It was in this house and in the frantic and bustling activity surrounding their father's work that the children grew up. The Jackson house, Jackie remembered, was something of a commune in the late 1960s and 1970s, with sets of people coming in to stay for periods of time while others were moving out.

One of the Jackson sons, Jonathan, remembered later that all kinds of children would show up with their parents—doctors, teachers, policemen, lawyers, and many others. When the children would ask Jonathan about his father's occupation, he did not know quite what to say. Jackson was not the usual preacher because he did not have a church. About the best Jonathan could do to explain his father's work was to say that he went around talking to people and trying to make their lives better.

Even Jackson's enemies conceded over the years that the atmosphere of the Jackson home and his work did nothing but encourage the graciousness, intelligence, and openness of each of the five. Santita, the eldest child, studied at Howard University in Washington, D.C.; worked as a congressional aide; and joined a vocal group backing up popular singer Roberta Flack. The youngest daughter, Jackie, attended college in Greensboro, where her parents had met. Jesse Jr., born while Jackson was with

Martin Luther King Jr. in Selma, got a master's degree in theology at the Chicago Theological Seminary and a doctorate in law from the University of Illinois before winning a seat in the U.S. House of Representatives. Jonathan, the youngest son, received a master's in business administration at Northwestern University and worked in a Chicago law firm. Yusef graduated from the exclusive St. Albans school in Washington, D.C., and then received a football scholarship to attend the University of Virginia. He became president of the Citizenship Education Fund, and both he and Yusef later ran an Anheuser-Busch distributorship.

Many folks in the Chicago community regarded Jesse and his organization as something like an extended family. PUSH attracted eager and joyous crowds to its weekly prayer meetings. Jackson launched a radio program to spread the word. From 9:00 A.M. to 12:00 P.M. on Saturday mornings, thousands listened to Jackson spread his social gospel through music, guest speakers, and his own charm and wit. Most of his Chicago listeners knew the chant by heart:

> I am—somebody!
> I may be poor, but I am—somebody!
> I may be on young, but I am—somebody!
> I may be on welfare, but I am—somebody!
> I may be small, but I am—somebody!
> I am—somebody!

Jackson even appeared on the Children's show *Sesame Street* and, with children from all races scattered around the set, recited along with them his free-verse poem.[5]

When Jackson began to learn the inside of the federal grant structure, he was able to tap several agencies for grant money to help launch various projects. And the successes continued. In 1972, both Schlitz Breweries and General Foods came to agreements (PUSH called them "covenants") to increase black labor, to purchase products produced by black-owned businesses, and to invest in black banks.

Jackson used his increasing connections with deft skill. When Coca-Cola balked at agreeing to PUSH's suggestions, Jesse invoked the name of comedian Bill Cosby, already a spokesman for the company, who was a strong supporter of Jackson. Coca-Cola agreed to a covenant.

Many of the agreements negotiated by Jackson and his organization were small, affecting only a few businesses. When Jackson was questioned why he settled in certain instances for nearly token agreements, he pointed out that the total impact of all the agreements already made and those that would be made in the future would dramatically change how the black business community saw itself and the influence it wielded. As the number of corporations that signed on continued to increase, such giants as Seven Up, Avon Products, and Quaker Oats, PUSH did begin to exert a national influence.

With each new agreement, the power of Jackson and his organization also grew. Hundreds of black-owned banks and black-owned corporations now became contributors to PUSH. They were all a family, Jackson would point out, and all had to show mutual support.

CHALLENGING DALEY

With Jackson's rise to prominence and power, with his confrontations on the civil rights front and then in the economic realm, he was honing skills that would make him a formidable figure in another arena far more national in scope than even his successes with PUSH—politics. Jackson and his organization, in mobilizing black ministers and black civic leaders, were throwing down a challenge to the political status quo in Chicago. To make the organization a viable, dynamic force for social change in Chicago and beyond, it had to shake up one of the most entrenched systems of city control in the United States. It was called the Daley machine.

Born in 1902 in Chicago's South Side Irish Catholic neighborhood of Bridgeport, Richard J. Daley methodically worked his way up the Cook County political ladder, holding several elected offices in state and city government before becoming mayor of Chicago in 1955. Father of seven children, gregarious, he was reelected five times, his political longevity nurtured by the careful distribution of jobs and influence. He was the consummate big-city machine mayor with a viselike grip on power.

The preeminent city boss of post–World War II America, Daley was an avowed segregationist whose own home neighborhood stood as a bastion against open housing. Nevertheless, Daley needed support of black voters to stay in office. They were a vital part of his Democratic power base. Indeed, in his two closest mayoral races, blacks provided him with his winning margins. Daley could maintain black support essentially because these voters had few other options. Republican challengers promised little. In addition, Daley's token support of groups of black ministers and local black politicos gave him enough leverage to maintain his political stranglehold.

When Martin Luther King Jr. had brought his civil rights struggle to Chicago, Daley had treated him and the SCLC in the same manner that he had treated his black constituency in Chicago. King had left Chicago with no concrete success in combating segregated housing, segregated public schools, and other social ills. In the wake of riots and looting in Chicago following King's assassination, Daley had issued a shoot-to-kill order for the black ghettos, an action few blacks ever forgot.

Jackson's arrival in Chicago presented Richard Daley with a political quandary. Here was a forceful leader bent on stirring the black community toward independent action. Here was a figure beginning to inspire loyalty and commitment never before manifested in the black South Side wards that Daley needed to hang on to power but into which he rarely traveled.

Daley had grown up in Bridgeport at a time when thousands of blacks from the rural South moved to the urban North. One and a half million southern blacks made their way north by the early 1920s to cities such as Detroit, Cleveland, and New York. However, the city that lured the most was Chicago, hub of the railroads and a place where a booming economy during World War I created a need for factory workers and other positions that poor blacks could take on. The black population increasingly concentrated on the city's South Side, an area roughly from 26th Street south to 55th Street. As the city continued to increase in size through the years, the area of black residences extended into western parts of the city. Nevertheless, it continued to be separate and less affluent, its residents confined not only geographically but socially and economically as well.

Although this so-called Black Belt provided Chicago's blacks with a measure of control over their own lives, the area quickly became increasingly overcrowded and poor, with high illness and mortality rates. Through the years, as the concentration of people increased and the jobs declined, a high percentage of residents were forced on relief. The ghetto was born and with it high crime rates, overcrowded schools, and a lack of parks and other recreational areas.

It was Daley's political dexterity that had enabled him to maintain enough loyalty from the black voting bloc to stay in power while, at the same time, he continued to resist basic social change that would distinctly improve the lives of Chicago's blacks. For blacks, the Daley machine was something of a plantation. The machine dispensed jobs by making certain that city contractors hired black workers. Daley's aldermen patrolled their districts, looking after their welfare checks, making sure medical care was available, and helping them out of trouble.

Jackson and his organization, slowly but inexorably, began to fracture that paternalistic feeling that Daley had cultivated for more than three generations. Jackson was now telling those in the black community that they could challenge the system that confined them in the ghetto, that limited their economic and educational opportunities, and that treated them as less worthy human beings.

From his Saturday morning pulpit at PUSH headquarters to his live radio program heard by hundreds of thousands at various PUSH-sponsored events around the city, Jesse's mutual identification with Chicago's blacks tightened. From the music to the revivalist-style preaching, from the successful challenges to the economic and political structure, Jackson was proving his mettle with the black constituency. In addition, he slowly moved into activities that were directly political in nature.

He began to conduct voter registration drives, not only encouraging blacks to register but also conducting sessions on how they could resist automatically pulling the lever for Democratic candidates and split their tickets depending on the stand various candidates took on the issues. He tried both to get them to turn out at the polls and to help them become sophisticated voters.

Jackson began increasingly to talk about political issues in the city, from school board races to specific races for aldermen. He called local reporters from the various city newspapers at all hours of the night to offer opinions and give suggestions about political matters. He occasionally showed up at Mayor Daley's office and sometimes would get an audience. Generally, he became an increasingly painful and bothersome irritant to the mayor.

By 1966, political observers could see the effects. The black vote for Daley began to drop. And in the 1968 presidential election, the 12 black wards of Chicago gave Daley 100,000 fewer votes than expected.

By the time of the 1972 Democratic National Convention in Miami Beach, Florida, Jackson was ready to put his guerilla campaign against the forces of Daley on full view of a national television audience. Dressed in a striped African shirt and wearing an Afro haircut and long sideburns, the mercurial Jackson challenged the Cook County delegates who were seated at the convention by questioning their credentials.

Roaming the convention floor to grant interviews to television reporters, Jackson even managed to persuade convention officials to allow him to make a speech. In glowing oratory, Jackson declared that young people, women, and African Americans were underrepresented at the convention. Although the battle with Daley at the convention had little national consequence at the time, it put Daley on notice that there was another powerful political force in the city of Chicago and that he was entirely unafraid to go toe to toe with the mayor. It also signified Jackson's growing fascination with political intrigue and combat.

A year earlier, at an event for black politicians held in Gary, Indiana, Jackson delivered the keynote address. In remarks to several thousand participants, Jackson railed about the two-party political structure in the United States in which the Democratic Party, favored by most blacks, had begun to take concerns over poverty, equal rights, available housing, and other issues for granted and in which the Republican Party had little concern at all for those issues. What the country needed, Jackson declared, was a party for blacks, and in Jesse's ever-active imagination, there was no question, no question at all, who would be the man to lead it.

PUSH EXCEL

By the mid-1970s, despite the many successes of Jackson and his organization, the financial ship was barely afloat. His many projects had spiraled in various directions, most of them into debt. The number of staff members hired by the organization increased beyond its means to pay. Some staffers worked for periods of time as volunteers. The organization had never operated under a carefully controlled budgetary process; instead, it mirrored the impulsiveness and flamboyance of its founder. It was always nearly out of control.

In 1976, Jackson launched a special program called Push for Excellence, or PUSH EXCEL. The initiative financially rescued the Jackson organization. Designed to unite parents, students, and teachers in a common drive toward educational excellence, it sought to reverse in the black ghettos the growing problems of drug abuse, teenage pregnancy, crime, and high school dropout rates. To his enemies and even unbiased observers, PUSH EXCEL seemed to many a Jackson aberration. Here was the controversial, fiery black preacher and activist, always in the posture of challenging the power structure, now in the position of advocating a program whose goals almost everyone could support.

Through PUSH EXCEL, Jackson spoke for the rights of each child to receive a free, quality education regardless of where the child lived. He saw it as an inspirational program appealing to black children to resist the lures that waited to entrap them and to prove their worth in ways that count. Its emphasis was on hard work, delayed gratification, and self-reliance.

In many ways, Jackson was mounting a movement to challenge the circumstances in which he had grown up as a boy. Jackson never forgot his grade school years and the whites-only school he passed every morning as he headed on his long trek to a shabbier school for blacks.

The overall thrust of the program was simple. It challenged both students and their parents to elevate their expectations and increase their performance. It used such simple devices as pledge cards for parents, teachers, and students to devote themselves to academic achievement. At the same time, it encouraged students to register to vote, to put the knowledge gained in the schools to use not only in the workplace but also in the political arena, and to reach for that full citizenship available to all Americans regardless of their color. The image of a student with a diploma in one hand and a voter registration card in the other became a familiar symbol of PUSH EXCEL.

The response to his new program was overwhelming approval. When CBS-TV's 60 *Minutes* ran a major segment on Jackson's new self-help initiative, more than 3,000 letters bombarded Jackson's headquarters, almost all of them positive. In a segment recorded for 60 *Minutes*, Jackson declared to a mostly black audience, "You know, I look at a lot of these theories that many social workers come up with, like, now the reason the Negro can't learn is his daddy's gone, his momma is pitiful, there's no food in the refrigerator, it's rats all in his house...and that's the reason he can't learn. Then we go to school and the teacher—standing there reeling the guilties—says, 'These poor and pitiful Negroes got all these trials and tribulations. Now I have to stand up here and teach them how to read and write and count.' Well, if we can run faster, jump higher and shoot a basketball straighter off of inadequate diets, then we can read, write, count and think of those same diets. The challenge is mobility."[6]

On another occasion, he declared in his unique manner, "Children must know that it is not their aptitude but their attitude that will determine their altitude."[7]

In mounting this campaign, Jackson for a time put aside his confrontational tactics. Instead of working against the power structure, he enlisted its help. The Ford Foundation and other foundations and corporations responded. Pilot studies began in several cities. In Los Angeles, the program showed such initial promise that the city's board of education provided $400,000 for a full-scale program in its school system. The Department of Health, Education, and Welfare under the Democratic administration of Jimmy Carter quickly began supporting the program and prepared some 500 school districts across the country to work with Jackson in implementing some of his ideas. Within a few years, federal support for the program would swell to more than $6 million.

With the increased national attention directed at his new program, Jackson seemed to be everywhere—giving interviews on radio and television, speaking to groups gathered in large convention halls and in small schools, increasing his contacts with government officials and corporate heads, and solidifying his support among civil rights and social action groups. As always, he made new enemies along with new friends; never did he slow down. Conservative political opinion assumed that this was just one more Jackson strategic maneuver to get in the limelight. Interestingly, a number of more liberal commentators were particularly annoyed with the generally conservative pedagogical approach of the campaign and its emphasis of self-help. Whatever the reactions, one opinion poll conducted in the early 1970s indicated that Jackson was one of the most recognizable figures in the United States.

By the early 1980s, the novelty of PUSH EXEL had worn thin. As a new Republican administration under President Ronald Reagan took over the White House, the climate for federal support for such programs shifted dramatically. Instead of backing the program, the new administration investigated it and did find enough careless bookkeeping to insist that the Jackson organization return more than $1 million of the funds earlier provided by the federal government. However, PUSH EXCEL and other Jackson programs would continue to function, being resilient in the bad times and flourishing in the good. Like their founder, they always kept moving.

NOTES

1. *New York Times*, June 2, 1969.

2. Thomas Landess and Richard Quinn, *Jesse Jackson and the Politics of Race* (Ottawa, Ill.: Jameson Books, 1985), 63.

3. Marshall Frady, *Jesse: The Life and Pilgrimage of Jesse Jackson* (New York: Random House, 1996), 275.

4. Frady, *Jesse*, 270.

5. "'I Am—Somebody,' Is a Poem by Jesse Jackson," http://encyclopedia. thefreedictionary.com/I%20Am%20-%20.

6. Robert McClory, "Rev. Jackson's 'Push to Excel'...," *Illinois Issues* 11 (May 1978), http://www.lib.niu.edu/ipo/ii780508.html.

7. "Quotations from a Spellbinder," *Time*, July 10, 1978, 46.

Chapter 8

THE NATIONAL RAINBOW COALITION AND THE ELECTION OF 1984

"RUN, JESSE, RUN!"

In 1888, at the Republican National Convention in Chicago, famed abolitionist Frederick Douglass became the first African American to be nominated by a major political party for president. He received one vote. It was a symbolic gesture. In 1972, Democratic congresswoman Shirley Chisholm of New York became the first black person actually to seek the nomination of a national party when she entered several Democratic primaries. In 1984, the Reverend Jesse Jackson entered the presidential sweepstakes. Not surprisingly, Jackson was in the race to win.

Many black leaders were skeptical that this was the time for a black candidate to take on this challenge. Coretta Scott King, for example, thought that such an effort was premature. Others feared a white backlash at the polls with a black candidate serving to mobilize white conservatives. However, Jackson believed, as he told friends on several occasions, that the season had arrived for a black campaign. It would show, he believed, that the civil rights movement had not ended when blacks were free to move beyond the back of the bus; it was now time that they map the direction in which the bus was headed, even to the point of being its driver.

With his high-voltage oratory and gospel politics, Jackson would excitedly point to the freedom train coming but would warn that its riders needed to get on, register to vote, and turn out at the polls. Forty-two years old, mature enough to have weathered numerous political storms and young enough to marshal relentless energy, Jackson said over and over again that he was on a mission to uplift the boats stuck on the bottom, to stand up for a rainbow coalition of the dispossessed, left behind, and underrepresented. "If you want someone to feed the hungry," he said, "here am I. Send me! If you want someone to clothe the naked, here am I. Send me! If you want someone who can pull the nation together—black, white, brown, old, young—here am I. Send me!"[1]

A perceptive student of recent presidential elections, Jackson realized that voter apathy by blacks had grievously wounded Democratic candidates. In the 1980 presidential election, for example, Ronald Reagan defeated Jimmy Carter in Arkansas by 5,000 votes. At the same time, there were more than 85,000 unregistered blacks. In state after state, a similar pattern prevailed. Jackson believed that a black candidate who could arouse black voter interest could drive hundreds of thousands of new Democratic voters to the polls.

Jackson began appealing to a "Rainbow Coalition" of the disadvantaged and rejected from all races and backgrounds. This coalition would include those from the 6 million Hispanic, half a million Native American, 40 million poor white, and millions of female voters and would forge a mighty power bloc of individuals who had formerly been excluded from the political process. Jackson saw this ballot-box drive as an extension of the nonviolent human rights revolution begun by Dr. King, in this case fighting with ballots and not bullets.

As he began to draw increasingly large crowds, many saw in his possible candidacy their own expression of discontent with a political process that virtually ignored their interests. From Puerto Ricans in the upper West Side of New York to young Native Americans just leaving reservations for colleges, Jackson began to capture their imagination and their support. An overwhelming number of black clergymen openly announced their support and encouraged their congregations to register to vote. The cries of "Run, Jesse, run!" echoed from pulpits as well as political rallies.

DECLARING A CANDIDACY

On November 3, 1983, at the Washington, D.C., convention center, the 42-year-old Jackson told the buoyant crowd that filled the massive building, "I seek the presidency to serve the nation at a level where I can help restore a moral tone, a redemptive spirit and a sensitivity to the poor and dispossessed of the nation. I seek the presidency because I want this nation to again become the hope of the free world not merely because of the power of our armaments but because developing nations understand by our foreign policy and programs of aid that the inscription on the Statue of Liberty is true."[2]

Jackson charged that the Democratic establishment had been relatively spineless in dealing with the Reagan administration and intimidated by the president's personal appeal and the recent success of right-wing politicians who made a career of bashing social programs and help for the poor as creeping socialism. Because of Reagan and his bevy of conservative supporters in Congress, Jackson asserted, Democrats had lost focus, ignored people left out of the American mainstream, and abandoned its goals and commitments.

It was this political timidity that Jackson took on four-square. The Reagan agenda, Jackson charged, had aided the rich and the nation's military–industrial interests at the expense of those who could least afford it. Because of Reagan's policies, the country was increasingly divided, with the country club set and those in the gated communities shutting themselves and their responsibilities off from the rest of American society. He called the Reagan presidency "anti-black, anti-Hispanic, anti-civil rights, anti-human rights, anti-poor."[3]

A mile away from the mobbed Convention Center, at a social service agency called Bread for the City, Inc., a 53-year-old unemployed black woman who had spent this morning as well as many mornings before in a line waiting for food, said, "I never thought I'd live to see this day."[4]

Jackson made a symbolic journey to the Deep South, back to Selma, Alabama, site of the 1965 march to Montgomery. At the historic Brown Chapel Church, he recalled the days and nights the marchers gathered inside to plan for the marches and then to keep up their spirits and courage after the beatings inflicted by police. However, today, unlike two decades earlier, Jackson rode with a state police escort. "Each generation has its own call to greatness," he declared at Tuskegee Institute. "This generation must lift the ceiling so only the sky is the limit."[5]

When Jackson declared his candidacy, less than 1 percent of all chemists, engineers, geologists, physicists, and geologists were black. In addition, despite recent mayoral victories by black candidates in major cities, there were no black senators and only one black governor.

Now, however, with his status as presidential candidate, Jackson suddenly was in the presence of Secret Service agents assigned to guard him. For the agents as well as those around Jackson, this situation invariably led to moments both comedic and surreal. In the boisterous exuberance of the black churches and in the rallies, with the shouting and dancing and bear hugs, the patience of the agents, as they tried to keep track of Jackson and those surrounding him, was sorely tested. On a number of occasions, actual fistfights broke out between Jackson's own campaign handlers and the agents.

Nevertheless, Jackson, as well as anybody, knew the high-risk stakes of the game he was now in and knew that the work of the agents was critical. He was acutely aware of the dangers involved in his running for president. Almost immediately after his announcement, the notes and telephone calls came in, threatening him, his friends, and his family. For Jackson, who had marched with King through the South and through the streets of Chicago and who had seen the hate and fury in the eyes of mobs, who had seen the beatings of fellow marchers, and who had been at the Lorraine Motel and heard the shot that killed his hero, none of these threats was treated lightly. "It's a family concern," he said. "My children are not paranoid, but they are sensitive to the danger, the risk. Those with whom we've worked throughout the years, who have accepted high-risk ventures, have to face the very real possibility of violence. So it's always a matter for discussion and prayer and consideration before every major decision."[6]

SELF-APPOINTED DIPLOMAT

On December 4, 1983, less than a month after Jackson had declared for the presidency, two Navy AE-6 Intruder reconnaissance planes were shot down over Syria during a bombing raid against Syrian antiaircraft positions in Lebanon. The pilot was killed and the bombardier–navigator, Lieutenant Robert O. Goodman Jr., who was black, was taken prisoner and housed in a military prison in Damascus. As Goodman's captivity lengthened and the Reagan administration seemed unable, through its Mideast envoy Donald Rumsfeld, to secure Goodman's release, Jackson saw an opportunity. In 1979, Jackson had traveled briefly to the Middle East and had met Palestinian leader Yasser Arafat and Syria's president Hafez al-Assad. For Jackson, these brief meetings were enough. At a press conference on Christmas Day 1983, Jackson told the world that that whoever can act in this situation should act and that he was going to undertake a rescue mission. He would go to Syria.

Undertaking such an unauthorized diplomatic mission was almost bizarre in both its audacity and its ingenuity. Many in the administration and numerous media pundits charged that Jackson, in his quest for attention, was undermining government authority, perhaps even treading into illegal acts. Despite the outcries, Jackson knew otherwise. The meeting of a U.S. citizen with a foreign leader is not against the law, and Jackson boarded a plane for Damascus. Robert Goodman's mother saw him off at the airport. During several days of long discussions with Syrian officials and with President Assad in his villa north of Damascus, days in which Jackson would take time to visit refugee camps and mingle with the crowds, he convinced the Syrian leader that the release of Goodman would be in the best interest of Syria as well as for peace, a gesture of goodwill to impress the world of his country's good faith.

In Washington, Jackson and Goodman were granted something of a "hero's welcome" by crowds of well-wishers at the airport and even, grudgingly, by President Reagan at the White House. "All Americans," Reagan declared, "must be pleased that the Government of Syria has told our Ambassador that they have agreed to release Lieutenant Goodman as a result of the efforts of the Reverend Jesse Jackson. We are delighted that this brave young man will soon be united with his family and that his ordeal is over. We hope the Syrian Government will continue to work for peace in Lebanon so that all foreign forces—Syrian, Israeli, and the multinational force—can come home and allow that country to be united, independent, and sovereign once more."[7]

To those on the campaign trail who charged that Jackson had never had anything approaching diplomatic experience, the visit to Syria was his answer. It gave his candidacy a new visibility. Suddenly, he was no longer in the eyes of many a one-issue, civil rights candidate. He was suddenly and jarringly now making a case that he could be an honest broker in world conflicts. His next trip abroad—to Latin America—would not be long in coming.

THE "HYMIETOWN" REMARK

There are traps waiting for individuals such as Jackson who set themselves up as moral and spiritual leaders. For them, there can be serious consequences resulting from any moral or spiritual failings of their own. By his own supreme force of will and indomitable energy, Jackson had become a spokesman for inclusion, a preacher of equal rights and of coming together in mutual respect and love. In his stirring speeches about the Rainbow Coalition, he talked about an America made up, like a quilt, of many patches, colors, sizes, and fabrics, woven together by a common thread of humanity. Now, at the beginning of his campaign for the presidency, three weeks after he had secured the release of Robert Goodman, Jackson sat in a cafeteria in Washington's National Airport chatting with two black reporters. During the casual conversation about the upcoming New York primary, Jackson mentioned that "most attempts to disrupt this campaign have come from Jewish people." During the conversation, Jackson muttered the coarse slang words "Hymie" and "Hymietown," referring to the city's large Jewish constituency. Nineteen days later, in the middle of a story about Jackson's race for the White House, those words appeared in the *Washington Post*.[8]

It was as if a tornado had ripped through Jackson's campaign. Television and print journalists jumped on the words, politicians scrambled for cover, Jewish groups expressed outrage, and Jackson had no idea what to do. At first, he denied ever saying the words. Then he tried to brush aside the questions by saying that he had meant nothing offensive and that anything that was said was in the context of a private conversation. Some of Jackson's advisers suggested that he try to ignore the matter; others counseled an apology to get the matter behind him.

Finally, in late February, before national Jewish leaders in a Manchester, New Hampshire, synagogue, Jackson made an emotional speech. "However innocent and unintended, it was wrong," Jackson said. "I deeply regret any pain I might have caused at any time.... It was not in the spirit of meanness [but] an off-color remark having no bearing on religion or politics." He said that he was offering his candidacy to "ensure a continuing dialogue and relationship between blacks, Jews, and Hispanics...as brothers and sisters."[9]

Later in the campaign, Jackson again apologized. Indeed, over the course of his career, he would continue to apologize. But for the campaign of 1984, the damage was severe.

THE FARRAKHAN DILEMMA

Another political tempest was snapping at Jackson and the Democratic Party. It involved Minster Louis Farrakhan, the black separatist leader of the Nation of Islam movement, and his support for Jackson.

Born in 1933 in Roxbury, Massachusetts, Louis Eugene Wolcott was raised in a politically savvy household in which it was not uncommon to see such black progressive literature as *Crisis Magazine*, published by the NAACP, on the dining room table. Sensitive and extraordinarily musically talented, Louis, by age 13, had played violin with the Boston Civic Symphony. At age 14, he won a contest on the national radio program the *Original Amateur Hour*. For a time, he attended Winston-Salem Teachers' College in North Carolina before devoting full time to a career as a vocalist, violinist, and dancer. While performing in a show in Chicago called "Calypso Follies," the young entertainer was invited to attend the Nation of Islam's Saviours' Day Convention. It was this invitation that changed his life.

The black Muslims, headed by self-proclaimed prophet Elijah Muhammad, foresaw the death of an America run by whites and a time when the world would be in hands of blacks whose destiny is to rule. The philosophy is militantly hateful toward whites, especially Jews. It also preaches, on the other hand, such values as respect for women, reverence for the elderly, clean and healthy living, frugality, respect for property, and hard work—all in preparation for blacks to assume their rightful place as leaders.

Louis Wolcott changed his name to Louis X according to black Muslim tradition. The "X" meant "unknown" and echoed the belief that because of the international slave trade over the centuries, the black individual's true identity and heritage are unknowable. Later, Louis adopted the last name of Farrakhan and became a member of the Nation of Islam in 1955. Rising quickly in the ranks, Farrakhan became a national spokesman for Elijah Muhammad and the head of the Harlem Mosque.

In 1977, two years after the death of Elijah Muhammad, Farrakhan formed his own black Muslim sect and gained his own national following. By 1984, he was a nationally known fiery apostle of black nationalism. With his usual rousing oratory, Farrakhan proclaimed in a speech given March 11, 1984, "Some white people are going to live ... but [God] don't want them living with us. He doesn't want us mixing ourselves up with the slave master's children, whose time of doom has arrived."[10]

For Jackson, the Farrakhan phenomenon presented a special dilemma. On the one hand, Farrakhan and his supporters, hoping that any Jackson success would be a slap at the white power structure regardless of political party, were openly supportive of Jackson's candidacy. Farrakhan publicly endorsed Jackson's candidacy on March 11. Indeed, a number of black Muslims acted as bodyguards for Jackson during the presidential campaign. On the other hand, Farrakhan's pronouncements were becoming acutely embarrassing for Jackson.

In addition to Farrakhan's tirades against whites and his ruminations about a possible race war looming on the horizon, Farrakhan described Judaism as a "dirty religion" and charged that the United States was engaged in a "criminal conspiracy" in its support for Israel. Not surprisingly, Jackson came under increasing pressure to disavow Farrakhan's support and denounce his statements.

At first, Jackson tried to avoid the issue. As the pressure from the media and from fellow Democratic politicians and advisers escalated, Jackson finally relented. In late June, calling Farrakhan's comments "reprehensible" and "morally indefensible," Jackson said, "I will not permit Minister Farrakhan's words, wittingly or unwittingly, to divide the Democratic Party."[11]

Democrats everywhere breathed a sigh of relief. With President Reagan already a prohibitive favorite for reelection, the party did not need divisive racial hatred or a simmering tension between blacks and Jews to erode its chances further.

ON THE PRIMARY CAMPAIGN TRAIL

Jackson faced a series of primary elections around the nation. He and his entourage faced the prospect of campaigning early on in such diverse locations as New Hampshire, Florida, Michigan, Illinois, and South Carolina—days and nights of speaking and traveling, grueling tests of endurance and logistics. They faced these things in the fall of 1983 with little money.

From the beginning of the primary election season, Jackson depended on the generous support of black ministers across the country. They turned out crowds, donated money, found places for the candidate and his assistants to stay, and provided transportation. As Jackson moved from state to state and it became obvious that he had the drive and enthusiasm to keep going, other donors sent money. Nevertheless, the Jackson campaign ran mostly on the fuel of human emotion and passion. The candidate and his supporters saw this political race as a cause, and the candidate and his supporters had vital experience in fighting for causes.

With no primary opposition and with a comfortable lead in opinion polls, President Reagan could spend the summer and early fall of 1984 in an imposing posture of presidential authority. The Democrats, meanwhile, flailed at each other along the primary trail.

At the beginning of the Democratic primaries, the field had seven candidates. The principal contenders were Walter Mondale, former senator from Minnesota and vice president under Jimmy Carter, architect of an elaborate presidential campaign organization, and, by far, the most well financed of the Democratic candidates; Gary Hart, senator from Colorado, former campaign manager for Robert F. Kennedy in his ill-fated presidential campaign of 1968, and heir to many of Kennedy's supporters; and John Glenn, senator from Ohio and former astronaut, the first man to orbit the earth. The rest of the field included California Senator Alan Cranston, Florida Governor Reuben Askew, former presidential candidate George McGovern, Senator Ernest Hollings of South Carolina, and Jackson. After the first few primaries, the field had been winnowed to three—Mondale, Hart, and Jackson.

All three of the main Democratic candidates basically agreed on the major issues—cuts in defense spending, higher taxes on the rich, a freeze on nuclear testing, freedom of choice on the abortion issue, expansion of civil rights legislation, and increased support for social programs.

Although his own campaign was less about specific issues and more about emotion and spirit, Jackson's position on most matters was clearly liberal. He urged blacks to take more responsibility for their own communities and stressed the need for greater opportunities for inner-city youth, especially those who had succumbed to the lures of gangs. He urged parents, teachers, and the government not to turn their backs on those youngsters but to turn toward them offering challenges and hope. On the diplomatic front, he called for increased aid to African nations and expressed sympathy for the plight of Palestinians.

Mondale, as expected, prevailed in Iowa with 49 percent of the vote. Nevertheless, the press concentrated on the less known second-place finisher, Senator Gary Hart. This new fascination with the relatively unknown but attractive Hart propelled the senator to a victory in the New Hampshire primary. Hart again prevailed in Florida. With his successes, however, Hart now became the focus of media scrutiny. Suddenly, he faced character issues regarding his marriage and questions about why he had changed his name from Hartpence to Hart; he also faced increasing pressure to explain in greater detail his position on certain issues. Soon Mondale regained the upper hand, winning significant victories in the Michigan caucuses. He cruised to victories in New York, Pennsylvania, and Texas and, despite Hart's superior showing in the western states, had the nomination clearly in hand as the Democrats prepared to travel to San Francisco for their convention in July.

For Jackson, the experience of the primaries was at once triumphant and bittersweet. He turned out tremendous crowds on occasion and reveled in the adulation. He was well aware that his candidacy was historic.

Despite major campaign gaffes and a lack of money, Jackson won primary nominations in Virginia, South Carolina, Louisiana, and Washington, D.C. In New York, nearly 270,000 blacks voted, more than any election in the state's history. Also carrying nearly one-fourth of the Hispanic voters, Jackson altogether received 26 percent of New York's statewide total. In all, across the country he received 3.5 million votes, up to 2 million of whom were newly registered. He carried more than 40 congressional districts and received more than 20 percent of the total votes cast. When he got to the convention, he had finished third in delegates behind Mondale and Hart.

GADFLY DIPLOMACY

In late June 1984, Jackson headed to Latin America for another whirl at private foreign negotiations. Arriving in Panama, Jackson began a six-day tour that would take him to El Salvador, Nicaragua, and Cuba. The highlight of Jackson's personal odyssey to Latin America was a meeting with Cuban leader Fidel Castro. On board the candidate's chartered jet, 63 reporters avidly took notes while a number of Secret Service agents joined his campaign coterie. At each stop and in the air, Jackson held forth on issues ranging from U.S. policy regarding the Panama Canal to the possibilities of a Latin American–U.S. regional alliance.

In Havana, dressed in olive fatigues and smoking a cigar, Castro met Jackson at the airport. It now had been more than a quarter of a century since Castro and his guerrilla army ousted the Cuban dictator, Fulgencio Bastista, on New Year's Day 1959. Castro's hard-line Communist politics and his close ties with the Soviet Union had made him the target of several U.S. presidential administrations, but he had remained in power. Now he and Jackson talked for more than eight hours. When the meeting ended, Jackson boasted of an extraordinary accomplishment. The Jackson plane would return to the United States carrying an additional 48 passengers—22 Americans who had been jailed in Cuba, mostly on drug-related offenses, and 26 anti-Castro Cubans, most of whom who had languished in Cuban jails for many years.

Jackson called his trip to Latin America a "moral offensive." After the agreement by Castro to free prisoners, Jackson told reporters, "There was a lot of common understanding...a lot of experience in suffering and exploitation." Jesse said that he had talked to Castro at length about religion and had encouraged the Cuban leader to be more positive in his approach to the church. As the plane with the new passengers prepared to leave Havana, one of the stewardesses noticed a startling coincidence. "There's a rainbow on the left side of the plane," she said. In stirring up political storms, it was if Jackson and his Rainbow Coalition had found a pot of gold.[12]

THE DEMOCRATIC NATIONAL CONVENTION

As he arrived in San Francisco for the Democratic National Convention, Jackson told supporters, "In 1964 we were trying to get in the convention and we only had chairs on the floor. Now we have a place on the stage. The rainbow coalition has actually taken hold."[13]

Not only had Jackson made a showing in the primaries far exceeding the expectations of most political observers, but he reached the convention with a measure of power the party had not expected him to achieve. Then he made the speech. "This is not a perfect party," he declared in one of the most memorable speeches in the history of American political conventions. "We are not a perfect people. Yet, we are called to a perfect mission: our mission to feed the hungry; to clothe the naked; to house the homeless; to teach the illiterate; to provide jobs for the jobless; and to choose the human race over the nuclear race. We are gathered here this week to nominate a candidate and adopt a platform which will expand, unify, direct and inspire our Party and the Nation to fulfill this mission. My constituency is the desperate, the damned, the disinherited, the disrespected, and the despised. They are restless and seek relief. They've voted in record numbers. They have invested faith, hope and trust that they have in us. The Democratic Party must send them a signal that we care. I pledge my best to not let them down."[14]

Andrew Young later wrote to Jackson that Martin Luther King Jr. would have been proud of him on that day.

Richard Hatcher, one of Jackson's closest advisers and an established black political figure in his own right, said, "There were a lot of things going on at that convention. For example, there was a lot of resistance on the part of the Democratic Party to—the whole idea, for example, of broad participation of minorities. Historically minorities have not participated in Democratic conventions to any significant degree. Well, Jesse Jackson changed all of that. He changed, the level—even the economic participation... the contracts at the convention. All of that changed because Jesse was a candidate and he was involved in those discussions."[15]

He was in it for the forgotten people, Jackson said. "Most poor children are neither black nor brown, they're white and they're female. Most poor people are not on welfare, they work every day. They work in fast-food restaurants, they clean hotels, they drive cabs, they do their labor in the dark, they're aides and orderlies in hospitals, they're cooks and janitors at schools, they keep other people's children, and ultimately cannot afford to take care of their own. Often they work in the football and basketball stadiums, selling the soft drinks and refreshments. But they are without health insurance. And they get sick too."[16]

For these people, Jackson would continue the quest.

LOOKING FORWARD

In early October, a study titled "Falling Behind: A Report on How Blacks Have Fared Under the Reagan Policies," issued by a nonpartisan study group, painted a grim portrait. In terms of income, poverty, and unemployment statistics, black Americans under the presidency of Ronald Reagan had fallen further behind. This was ammunition, if he needed any, for Jackson to launch a spirited attack on the Republican Party and its president for further dividing rich from poor, black from white. At a rally in early October in Memphis, Tennessee, Jackson, on the campaign trail with vice-presidential nominee Geraldine Ferraro, turned up his preacher's appeal: "We are told by Jesus Himself that you judge a tree not by the bark if wears, but by the fruit it bears … leadership is measured by how one treats the least of these that cannot help themselves."[17]

Reagan was easily reelected in November 1984. Americans were not inclined to turn out of office the personally affable president. However, Jackson's powerful presence in the campaign had broken new ground, pushing blacks closer to the center of political power in America. Jackson's candidacy and the work of his campaign team in registering voters contributed to the large black voter turnout in the 1984 election. An estimated 3 million blacks voters turned out at the polls in the Democratic primaries, and more than 10 million delivered their votes to Mondale in the general election, 90 percent of the black vote.

Jackson's campaign also launched careers for a number of young black political activists. Donna Brazile, Jackson's 23-year-old field director, later held key positions in the campaigns of Walter Mondale, Michael Dukakis, and Bill Clinton. She became the first black American campaign manager in Al Gore's extremely narrow loss to George W. Bush. Minyon Moore, who worked as a deputy field director for Jackson, later served as a White House public affairs director under Bill Clinton and held important leadership positions in the Democratic National Committee.

Looking back at the election, Jackson said that his campaign had blazed a trail—3.5 million votes—surprising not only all the political experts and pundits but also the people who made up the Rainbow Coalition. They never imagined it could happen, Jackson said. Now, renewed with both a sense of gratification and vindication as well as a sense of joy, Jackson was more confident than ever that he could bring people together. "I know that, in time, all that separates us from each other is information." When individuals from various ethnic, cultural, and racial backgrounds have access to each other, he said, barriers will fall. "To make progress we have to forgive each other, redeem each other, and focus on common ground."[18]

NOTES

1. "Jesse Jackson Shakes Up Race for White House," *U.S. News & World Report*, December 19, 1983, 35.

2. *Washington Post*, November 4, 1984.

3. *Washington Post*, November 4, 1984.

4. *Washington Post*, November 4, 1984.

5. *Washington Post*, November 5, 1984.

6. Doug Foster, "Jesse Jackson—He Thinks He Can Win," *Mother Jones*, October 1, 1987, http://www.motherjones.com/news/feature/1987/10/foster.html.

7. Federal Register Division, National Archives and Records Service, *Public Papers of the Presidents of the United States, Ronald Reagan*, 1984 (Washington, D.C.: U.S. Government Printing Office, 1956–), 1.

8. *Washington Post*, February 13, 1984.

9. *New York Times*, February 27, 1984.

10. Jay Rogers, "Louis Farrakhan," http://www.forerunner.com/forerunner/X0065_Nation_of_Islam.html.

11. "Stirring Up New Storms," *Time*, July 9, 1984, 10.

12. "Stirring Up New Storms," 8.

13. *New York Times*, July 16, 1984.

14. "Jesse Jackson: 1984 Democratic National Convention Address, delivered 18 July 1984, San Francisco," http://www.americanrhetoric.com/speeches/jessejackson1984dnc.htm.

15. Frontline, "Interview with Richard Hatcher," http://www.pbs.org/wgbh/pages/frontline/jesse/interviews/hatcher.html.

16. "Interview with Rev. Jesse Jackson, Civil Rights Leader," http://www.teenink.com/Past/9900/January/Interview.

17. *New York Times*, October 4, 1984.

18. Foster, "Jesse Jackson."

Chapter 9

"COMMON GROUND
AND COMMON SENSE"

A MATURING CANDIDATE

In 1984, Jesse Jackson had succeeded not only in making himself a national political figure but also, for the first time, in aggressively awakening the country to the possibility that a black candidate could seriously challenge in the presidential primary system. Now, in 1988, Jackson was ready to make a very determined run.

The old college quarterback looked to make big plays in this political season. No more symbolic breakthroughs now, he said; no more merely learning how to run. Those steps were behind him. He was ready seriously to compete. "Not as in place well, not as in good showing, not as in making a difference!" he shouted in a speech to New York union activists. "Not nothing like that! As in win. We can win!"[1]

Long gone now are the long hair and the African shirts. No longer does his rhetoric concentrate almost exclusively on civil rights issues. But he has not mellowed. At rallies, he is a veritable hurricane of energy. As a stump speaker, no other candidate can compare. For Jackson, this manic charge through towns and cities is not a chore. The handshaking, the embraces, the ebullient mixing—it is as if he cannot get enough of it. His aides constantly find themselves tugging on his coat sleeve to get him to wrap up rallies and move on to the next.

"In 1984 we were blazing a trail," he declared to a reporter. "We got 3.5 million votes, even from people who were in the throes of disbelief because they'd never imagined it could happen. Now, in 1987, you see strange combinations of ranchers, autoworkers, meat packers, steelworkers, teachers, and firemen—many of whom have been on the right—in co-alition with those who have been to the left: blacks, Hispanics, Asians."[2]

The same political problems that had bedeviled Jackson in his first run for president had not evaporated. His raw ambition, grating not only to his enemies but to many of his friends as well, was still on display. He was still inclined to exaggeration if not blatant misrepresentation. His campaign suffered on occasions from near chaos, even though he had a larger staff of campaign workers this time around working from the new "Jackson 88" headquarters in downtown Chicago. The disorganization prompted the legitimate question as to whether a candidate who could not manage his campaign well could manage the country. Nevertheless, his confidence was infectious. If through sheer will a candidate could make it all come together, then the black preacher–politician from Illinois had a fighting chance.

He especially wanted to avoid the squabbles and bickering that had disrupted his first campaign. Stick to the issues, he would tell his staff. "It's our message that people are listening to: Save the family farm, save jobs, save the environment, save the family, reinvest in America, down with drugs, up with hope. That's what we're saying. That's what people want to hear."[3]

He told reporters that his following was much larger than it had been in 1984. It carried with it a larger responsibility. "Last time my rhetoric was sufficient to do what I had to do—open up the process, demand room for progressive-thinking people, register new voters. You know there's a right wing and a left wing, and it takes both to fly a plane. My concern is about 85 million voters in neither wing: they're in the belly of the plane. If one perceives that some changes have taken place, they have. I do not resist growing. I do not resist maturing. I do not resist expanding."[4]

He was in the belly of that plane now, set to ride out whatever storms picked up in his journey, each day looking to convert new voters, to convince the doubters finally that he, Jesse Jackson, could actually pilot the country.

THE PRIMARY SEASON

Because President Ronald Reagan was completing his second four-year term in office, the 1988 presidential election would have no incumbent president running for reelection. Both parties, therefore, would have a wide-open primary election to replace Reagan. The clear favorite for the Republican nomination was Vice President George Bush of Texas, who had the full support of the president. A few challengers lined up to challenge Bush. They included Senator Robert Dole of Kansas; Pierre Du-Pont, former congressman and governor of Delaware; Alexander Haig, Reagan's former secretary of state; Jack Kemp, former National Football League quarterback and congressman from New York; and Pat Robertson, televangelist and founder of the Christian Coalition.

Although Senator Dole had early support, winning the Iowa Caucus, the nominee for the Republicans was Bush, who pledged a "kinder, gentler America" in an effort to appeal to a broad constituency of voters.

If the Republican primary elections had few surprises, the Democrats served up a number of unexpected results. In early 1987, Gary Hart, senator from Colorado, who had run strongly in the 1984 primary race, was the clear front-runner. Other Democratic candidates included Al Gore, senator from Tennessee; Michael Dukakis, governor of Massachusetts; Joseph Biden, senator from Delaware; Richard Gephardt, congressman from Missouri; Paul Simon, senator from Illinois; Bruce Babbitt, former governor of Arizona; and Jesse Jackson.

Early in the primary season, Gary Hart suffered through damaging revelations about his personal life, and his candidacy foundered. Biden's campaign also quickly became mired in controversy when it was learned he had plagiarized a speech written by a British politician. He dropped out of the race. Dukakis, Gore, and Jackson would soon dominate the Democratic field.

On the campaign trail, Jackson wheeled in and out of towns with an exuberance that few people had ever seen. Who was this dynamo from Chicago who had marched with Martin Luther King Jr.? What made him think that folks across the country would throw aside the entrenched tradition of white male presidents and vote for him? He was out to show that he understood their problems and needs. In Iowa Falls, Iowa, laid-off workers were reeling from a decision by Farmland Foods to close a packing plant. At a town square meeting, Jackson declared, "We must change the equation. There's no sense of corporate justice, of fairness." We'd better wake up and fight the "merger maniacs," he said.[5]

In Adair, Iowa, Jackson spoke to 800 people, an enormous crowd in the frigid cold of a midwestern winter. A dairy farmer named Dixon Terry later told a reporter, "Average folks turned out by the hundreds. Old folks were coming out to see the preacher preach, some were crying; he really touched a nerve."[6]

If Jackson could get to the people, he believed, if he could touch them, hug them, and speak to them, they would embrace his message. Even though he knew that the 1988 campaign, like the earlier one, would be plagued by a shortage of funds, he hoped that the organization could get out that message with more sophistication.

Part of the problem was Jackson himself. A number of his aides during both runs for the presidency later reported their disillusionment in working with the candidate, from imperious and angry outbursts regularly directed at them to his totally controlling personality. One of the staffers later lamented, "His constant unwarranted abuse and mostly unjustified criticism were beginning to wear me down."[7]

After a speech in Iowa, Jackson and his team were stranded on a runway without a phone, waiting for a plane they had forgotten to book. They were two hours late for one meeting and would have to cancel another. An exasperated Jackson gathered his troops and wailed about the incompetence. "I've had enough of this 'Well, I tried, but he lied, so we died,' excuses. As soon as we get to 'we died' it doesn't matter if you tried or he lied because we are all dead already.'" When he finished the odd sentence, the sternness wilted into a knowing smile, and he quipped to a friend, "When I get the idea, the words they just come."[8]

This was Jackson on the campaign trail—a bewildering mixture of surliness and moments of eloquence.

The words just came. "Mention the name of any other candidate and you don't generate enough electricity to light a refrigerator bulb," said Democratic pollster Peter Hart. "Mention Jesse Jackson and the energy fills the room."[9]

At one campaign stop, Jackson was firing up the troops to get out and vote. He talked about grasshoppers. "They wallow in the grass. They change color with the grass.... They're scared of shoes. They panic when they hear lawnmowers." His people, he says, are not grasshoppers. They are giants. The crowd is in full force, yelling, "Right on, Jesse!" "Giants should not be wallowing in the grass...and dodging the wind. Running from shoes. Panicking when they hear lawnmowers. Giants must stand tall, act tall, and behave tall."[10]

At another, he spoke about uniting disadvantaged whites and blacks. "If we turn to each other, and not on each other, we the people, we are the majority. We can win."[11]

Jackson seemed to be making progress toward that multiracial coalition. At a rally sponsored by the United Auto Workers in Kenosha, Wisconsin, where Chrysler Corporation was in the process of closing its plant, a reporter spotted a middle-age white woman leaning on a crutch, wearing a hooded sweatshirt with the words "Black to the Future."

Later, at another rally in rural Wisconsin, this one in a huge barn that had often been used for jamborees and hoedowns, a crowd made up of mostly white farmers and their families gathered to hear the famous preacher politician. Most were drawn by the spectacle not from any admiration for Jackson. What happened inside was telling. One reporter who had been at Jackson rallies in several cities was astonished. "Parents held up children to see, blond teenage girls giggled over his good looks, skeptics were drawn in, and by the end of the address, the crowd was chanting, 'Win, Jesse, win! Win, Jesse, win!'"[12]

In Beaumont, Texas, a man named Bruce Hill approached Jackson. He had seen Jackson on another occasion, Hill said. It was at the Selma, Alabama, civil rights march. Hill told Jackson that he was also marching that day—only he was not marching with the civil rights demonstrators; he was marching for the Ku Klux Klan. Over the years, all that had changed. Hill said, "I was young and full of it. I've changed. Just like a lot of us ole Southern boys. Jesse Jackson is right on the issues as far as the working-man is concerned." How many more Bruce Hills were out there? Jackson was determined to bring them forth.[13]

SUPER TUESDAY AND BEYOND

After early losses in Iowa and New Hampshire, Jackson faced a day of reckoning in the 1988 campaign, the day called "Super Tuesday" by the media. On March 8, there were 20 state primaries races, two-fifths of the total number of states. This day would make or break a number of candidates.

For Jackson, Super Tuesday solidified his candidacy. He won five southern states—Alabama, Georgia, Louisiana, Mississippi, and Virginia. More than one-fourth of the Democratic voters nationwide selected Jackson. Four days later, he won the caucus in his birth state of South Carolina. Jackson then headed to Illinois.

Much of history can be glimpsed merely by images. In 1968, when Martin Luther King Jr., along with hundreds of marchers including Jackson, had walked the streets of Cicero, Illinois, the tough working-class suburb of Chicago, they had been pelted with rocks and called every racial slur imaginable. Photographers had snapped photographs of the angry crowd as it pressed in on King. He later said he had never been so terrified by hatred. That is one image.

Two decades later, Jackson was back in Cicero. There is another image. Jackson was talking about economic justice. Standing around him were workers, almost all of them white, from the Sheet Metal Workers' Union Local 571, carrying signs that read "Jesse, Help Us Save Our Jobs." Cicero had been hit with the news that General Electric planned to move its local operations to Alabama, where there was no union. Al Carabello, secretary of the local union, had given Jackson a check for $5,000. "No other candidate has even been here," said Carabello.[14]

For Jackson, this is the kind of response he had sought from the beginning of the campaign—forging a coalition of those who were economically struggling and finding common ground regardless of race. Throughout the campaign, he had used the phrase "economic violence" to capture the distance between those to practice it, from the government to the corporations to those who suffer from it.

On March 15, Jackson finished second in Illinois. More than two decades earlier, as a first-year college student in the state, he had quit school and returned disillusioned to the South. He had come an extraordinary distance.

On March 26, Jackson achieved a stunning victory against Dukakis in Michigan, winning 55 percent of the vote. Along with his strong showing in the South on Super Tuesday, this impressive win in Michigan shook not only political prognosticators but also the Democratic Party. The realization that Jackson was in position actually to win the nomination jolted many voters. No longer was this a quixotic adventure.

What if Jackson actually did win the nomination? What ruinous effects for the Democratic Party would his candidacy have not only in the race for president but also for congressional races and even for state and local races? Opinion polls throughout the spring of 1988 indicated that less than 40 percent of whites in the United States would likely vote for Jackson in a November match with George Bush. Even among white Democrats, less than 50 percent indicated a willingness to support Jackson. Given these sentiments, could Jackson continue his startling early momentum?

The next big test came in Wisconsin, a politically progressive state with a large working population in Milwaukee. Wisconsin also had a fairly sizable minority population even though the state was mainly rural. Jackson expected to do well in Wisconsin. His campaign stops around the state were encouraging, even in mostly white, farming areas. However, the staff assigned to Wisconsin was largely inexperienced. With poor scheduling decisions and other organizational snafus, Jackson's message was drowned in missteps and misunderstandings. He limped out of Wisconsin with a second-place finish and headed to New York.

The New York primary, scheduled for April 19, was crucial. Any possibility that Jackson might seriously contend for the presidential nomination at the Democratic convention or be seriously considered as a vice-presidential candidate rested on a New York victory. The Jackson team was confident.

As the Jackson caravan worked its way through New York State from Rochester toward New York City, the candidate drew large crowds. These were mostly white audiences, and they were enthusiastic. Nevertheless, as Jackson and the team approached New York City, the high spirits waned with the news stories from the major city papers.

Although Jackson, throughout his career, successfully used the press to advance his own agendas and to stir up attention, he always displayed an air of combativeness when dealing with reporters. At press conferences, he barely tolerated confusing or antagonistic questioning. He often accused news organizations of creating stereotypes in stories about the poor and disadvantaged. He also attacked newspapers, radio and television, and other news outlets for not hiring minority workers.

In New York City, the press corps relished the chance to skewer any public figure who displayed impatience or hostility in the press arena. Jackson was a special target. They attacked him for his audacious visit to Fidel Castro in Communist Cuba, they questioned his lack of experience in governing, and they especially zeroed in on his problems arising from the infamous "Hymietown" remark during the 1984 campaign. In addition, New York City Mayor Ed Koch seemed fixated on making sure Jackson did not carry the state of New York. Early in the campaign, he said that any Jew who voted for Jackson had to be crazy. The New York press gave Koch every opportunity he wanted to repeat the intemperate remark. One Jackson supporter swore that he saw Koch on television at least once every day blasting Jackson.

Meanwhile, Dukakis was now riding high. With a capable organization, a financial war chest, and the support of most of the Democratic officials and politicians, he arrived in New York as the prohibitive favorite. His credentials were now clearly defined: executive ability, organizational acumen, and an enviable record of success as the governor of a major state.

Jackson carried New York City on election day; he did not carry all of New York State. Dukakis won 51 percent of the vote statewide, and Jackson had 37 percent. The Jackson forces were dispirited. In the ballroom of the New York Sheraton Hotel, there was much carping about what went wrong. The state that could have launched the Jackson candidacy nearly in orbit was instead the one that put the final clamps on any chance he might have had to win the nomination. However, when Jackson walked in the ballroom to make his obligatory concession speech, he seemed above the anger that was so palpable around him. He congratulated Dukakis for running a clean campaign and said that the president must make the country better, not bitter, and that president would be Dukakis. "We cannot become cynical, we have come too far," Jackson said. "From Rosa Parks in Montgomery, Alabama, to this ballroom, we have come a long way. We know this road. We will keep going. We must keep hope alive."[15]

Jackson was less a victim of his mistakes than the fact that most voters did not believe that he was ultimately capable of winning the presidential election. As in 1984, he could not attract enough working-class whites to fill out his coalition of the economic disadvantaged. Still, nearly 7 million people voted for him nationwide in the primary elections, about 3 million fewer than voted for Dukakis.

As the second-place finisher, Jackson believed he should have a strong claim for the vice-presidential nomination. Instead, Dukakis, shortly before the convention, announced that Lloyd Bentsen, senator from Texas, would join him on the ticket.

Shortly after Dukakis had made his selection of Bentsen as the vice-presidential nominee, Jackson supporters gathered to hear their candidate at the Missionary Baptist Church in Nashville, Tennessee. There was a mixture of pride and anger in the air—pride because of Jackson's achievement of becoming the first serious candidate for president and anger that he was left off the ticket. A 23-year-old black supporter named Steven Waters said to a reporter, "Jesse represented us, and we don't want him to be refused a place on the ticket just because he's a black man." Waters held a sign that said, "No Jesse, No Rainbow Coalition, No Democratic Victory."[16]

As Jackson and others prepared to travel to Atlanta for the convention, the message on Steven Waters's sign in Nashville put very succinctly the problem facing the party. Democratic leaders from Dukakis on down knew that America was not ready to elect a ticket with a black on it. They did not need opinion polls to tell them that.

Nevertheless, black voters remained a vital ingredient in any Democratic recipe for success at the ballot box in November. Any defection of that voting bloc because of anger that Jackson would not be named to the ticket would spell doom for the party.

THE CONVENTION

One by one, Dukakis's opponents had peeled away during the various primary elections until, by the time of the convention in Atlanta, only

Jackson was left as a declared candidate still in opposition to Dukakis. The Massachusetts senator, nevertheless, held an insurmountable lead. He won on the first ballot, receiving 2,876 votes. Jackson garnered 1,218.

By any measure, Jackson had achieved an extraordinary measure of success, and when it was his turn to take over the microphone at the convention, so did his family. Indeed, *Newsweek* magazine ran a headline titled "'Proud to Be Jacksons': Jesse's Kids Steal the Show at the Convention." Each of the five children, beginning with the youngest, 13-year-old Jacqueline, stepped forward to the television cameras to say a few words before Jesse addressed the convention. Jesse Jr., destined himself for a political career, said, "I am sure that the children in the King family are proud to be Kings. And I'm sure the children in the Kennedy family are proud to be Kennedys. But we the children of Jesse and Jacqueline Jackson are proud to be Jacksons." Jesse Jr. said that his father exemplified the advice that he had given to all his children—tragedy is not in failing but in aiming low.[17]

Jackson's emphasis on his family at the convention in many ways followed a path blazed by comedian Bill Cosby on his long-running television show. Cosby and his fellow actors captured on screen the everyday experiences of a black family—Dr. Cliff Huxtable, a physician; his wife Clair, an attorney; and their five children. The upper-middle-class Huxtables were intelligent and witty and had high values and strong bonds. American television viewers embraced the family. The Cosby show was the most popular TV series from 1985 to 1988.

Now, at the Democratic National Convention, Jackson introduced his real-life, all-American black family. It is not coincidental that Bill Cosby was a strong supporter of Jackson and appeared with him at events throughout the campaign.

Jackson called his convention address "Common Ground and Common Sense." As he did in 1984, Jackson was a spokesman for the forgotten. "I know they work," he declared, "I'm a witness. They catch the early bus. They work every day. They raise other people's children. They work every day. They clean the streets. They work every day. They change the beds you slept in these hotels last night and can't get a union contract. They work every day. They work in hospitals. I know they do.... No job is beneath them, and yet when they get sick, they cannot lie in the bed they made up every day. America, that is not right. We are a better nation than that. We are a better nation than that.... The only justification we have for looking down on someone is that we're going to stop and pick them up."[18]

IN RETROSPECT

Jackson worked hard to support the Democratic ticket, which eventually lost to George Bush and his vice-presidential candidate, Dan Quayle, a senator from Indiana. The political tides were not yet ready to wash away the Republican hold on the White House.

In his presidential run in 1988, Jackson galvanized black voters, millions of whom he had helped register prior to the election; he raised important social and racial issues on the national level; and, for the first time, he legitimized the possibility that an African American could win the nation's highest office.

Many defeated political candidates fade from public view. There would never be any such fading of Jackson. In an emotional speech at Harvard University, he sounded the call for new leadership in America, praising the liberal tradition that had produced such giants as John F. Kennedy. For two hours, Jackson enthralled a standing-room audience of 600, recalling that such progressive reforms as child labor laws, civil and women's rights legislation, and collective bargaining were all products of progressive men and women dedicated to improving the lot of all citizens. Conservatives, by contrast, he said, stood for monopolies, imperialism, and big business. "I am a liberal," Jackson declared, "a liberator and change agent."[19]

His own personal campaign continued.

NOTES

1. Doug Foster, "Jesse Jackson—He Thinks He Can Win," *Mother Jones*, October 1, 1987, http://www.motherjones.com/news/feature/1987/10/foster.html.

2. Foster, "Jesse Jackson."

3. Elizabeth O. Colton, *The Jackson Phenomenon: The Man, the Power, the Message* (New York: Doubleday, 1989), 61.

4. Foster, "Jesse Jackson."

5. Andrew Kopkind, "A Populist Message Hits Home," *The Nation*, July 18–25, 1987, 55.

6. Kopkind, "A Populist Message Hits Home," 53.

7. Colton, *The Jackson Phenomenon*, 175.

8. "The Guardian Profile: Jesse Jackson," *Afrocentric News*, http://www.afrocentricnews.com/html/jackson_profile.html.

9. "Jackson's Big Takeoff," *Newsweek*, April 11, 1988, 22.

10. Joyce Purnick and Michael Oreskes, "Jesse Jackson Aims for the Mainstream," *New York Times Magazine*, November 29, 1987, 34.

11. "Day of the Preachers," *Newsweek*, March 7, 1988, 45.

12. Stanley Crouch, "Beyond Good and Evil: The Paradoxes of Jesse Jackson," *The New Republic*, June 20, 1988, 20.

13. Colton, *The Jackson Phenomenon*, 106.

14. "The Power Broker," *Newsweek*, March 21, 1988, 18.

15. Stanley Crouch, "Beyond Good and Evil: The Paradoxes of Jesse Jackson," *The New Republic*, June 20, 1988, 20.

16 "Jackson: The Fire This Time," *Newsweek*, July 25, 1988, 18.

17. "'Proud to Be Jacksons': Jesse's Kids Steal the Show at the Convention," *Newsweek*, August 1, 1988, 21.

18. "Common Ground and Common Sense," delivered by Reverend Jesse Jackson at the 1988 Democratic National Convention, Atlanta, Georgia, http://teacher.scholastic.com/researchtools/articlearchives/honormlk/spjackso.htm.

19. Paula Maute, "Jackson at Harvard, Calls for Bold Leadership," http://www.tech.mit.edu/VI109/N21/jackso.21n.html.

Chapter 10

KEEPING A NATIONAL VOICE

POLITICAL DRIFT

At the 1988 Democratic National Convention in Atlanta, Jesse Jackson was at the pinnacle of his political career. Although he campaigned in the general election with some vigor for the Democratic nominee, Michael Dukakis, and vice-presidential nominee, Geraldine Ferraro, the ticket lost decisively.

Jackson had actively sought the presidency for more than four years through two presidential elections. He had achieved a degree of success for a black candidate unparalleled in American history. Many of his supporters still harbored hopes that Jackson, despite his race, despite the controversies he had generated, could actually win the Democratic nomination in another four years.

Buffeted by conflicting advice, emotions, and personal aspirations, Jackson made a crucial decision following the 1988 election—he would not continue his active campaigning for the presidency. The physical demands of the hectic whirl of endless speeches and campaign stops had drained the nearly indefatigable Jackson. The prospect of constant fundraising, the grueling battles with the press and with the other candidates, and the thankless bickering over the campaign organization had taken its toll.

The desire to make a difference, the lures of the limelight, and his personal sense of destiny still tugged hard. He would channel all of it in a different direction.

Following the 1988 election, he moved his home from Chicago to Washington, D.C., leaving behind Operation PUSH for others to run, at least for a time. In Washington, he would be in the midst of the power brokers and the decision makers, surrounded by every conceivable media outlet. Many Washington observers assumed that his presence in the city signaled Jackson's intent to mount a new social action campaign centered in the nation's capital; others guessed that Jackson eyed the position of mayor of the District of Columbia, a position from which he could wield political power and gain additional attention.

When Washington's longtime mayor Marion Barry was forced out of office by a drug scandal in early 1990, Jackson was considered one of the top contenders for the job, a near certain winner if he chose to run. He decided against it. Instead, he announced in July 1990 that he would seek election as the District of Columbia's "statehood senator," a position recently established by the city to advocate statehood for the District.

Residents of the District of Columbia have the dubious distinction of being the only citizens of the United States without full representation in the U.S. Congress. The U.S. Constitution gave Congress exclusive legislative jurisdiction over the District; thus, no voting member of Congress represents the city. The situation is a constitutional anomaly that residents, since the early 1970's, have struggled to change, many pushing for formal statehood.

Jackson was elected in November 1990 and sworn into office in January 1991. The position was popularly known in Washington as "shadow senator" since it carried no voting power in Congress. Jackson relished the idea of having access to Congress and the trappings that the job brought with it. He did not relish the notion that he would in any way be a "shadow." Jackson accepted the responsibilities of the job, did what he could to persuade Congress to adopt legislation granting statehood to the District of Columbia, and used the position as a pulpit to bring to light the needs of the city and the ways in which Congress had failed to provide them. Nevertheless, the job, with so little authority and with a cause so little in favor outside of Washington, was in many ways a thankless one. Jackson did not seek reelection after the end of one six-year term.

This was a time for channeling his mercurial ambition, a time to find clear direction for the Rainbow Coalition, the multiracial group of people and causes that had come to his side in his runs for the presidency. He hoped to build an effective progressive political coalition that could affect the country's direction for years to come. Its exact political role was not yet clear to Jackson. It might serve as the foundation for a third political party. It might be the nucleus of a powerful pressure group working within the Democratic Party. It might be an independent lobbying force exerting pressure on Congress on a variety of issues from homelessness to drug abuse. It might be used to mobilize voters. Or it might be a combination of all of those things. The challenge was to keep the fervor and excitement alive among those who had given so much to the cause, to convince those who had supported him over the years to keep the faith that his efforts and theirs could make a difference. Jackson would continue to speak for the causes of these people and look for opportunities to advance their causes.

Nevertheless, the career of Jesse Jackson has consistently been marked by the unexpected, the dramatic, the chance to capture the limelight and step into the breach. In the summer of 1990, the actions of Iraqi strongman Saddam Hussein gave Jackson his next opportunity.

PERSONAL DIPLOMACY: IRAQ AND SADDAM HUSSEIN, 1990

In the early hours of the morning of August 2, 1990, more than 100,000 troops of the army of the Middle Eastern country of Iraq invaded the neighboring Gulf state of Kuwait. Following a series of disputes over oil rights and other issues between the two countries, Iraqi President Saddam Hussein ordered his forces across the border. Within 24 hours, all of Kuwait was under Iraqi control. With startling speed and audacious force, the Iraqis soon established a provisional government.

Since 1979, Hussein had ruled Iraq with a cunning hand, fending off any challenges to his leadership with unstinting ruthlessness. He held this country of vast distance and diverse ethnic and religious groups together with violence and the fear of violence. In maintaining his dominant hold on power, Hussein had even resorted to the use of chemical weapons to put down a revolt of the Kurdish population in northern Iraq. He had razed Shi'ia (a branch of Islam) towns and killed thousands in maintaining power in the south.

Normally content to glory in his autocratic rule, Hussein had once before attempted conquest in an ill-advised attack on Iran that led to a costly, protracted war. Even after that ignominious venture, he remained determined to put Iraq at the forefront of the Arab world. The attack on Kuwait was sudden but not all that surprising. It was now clear that Iraq represented a growing threat to the region and to the world's supply of oil.

Almost immediately following the invasion, the UN Security Council denounced the actions of Iraq, imposed sanctions, and demanded that Iraq withdraw its troops. Ignoring the demands, Hussein announced that Kuwait had been annexed as a province of Iraq. In backing up the announcement, he moved thousands of troops to within striking distance of Saudi Arabia, a major source of oil for the United States. President George Bush was convinced that the ultimate intention of Saddam Hussein was, indeed, to invade oil-rich Saudi Arabia, and the president began to organize a multinational coalition to repel Iraq's moves. The mission of the coalition was to free Kuwait from the clutches of Iraq as well as to ensure that Hussein was thwarted in any further advance on Saudi Arabia and U.S. oil interests. Within the space of several weeks, U.S. bombs would fall on Baghdad and other Iraqi cities.

Meanwhile, thousands of foreign nationals, including large numbers of Americans, British, and French, who were in Kuwait at the time of the invasion found themselves trapped, unable to flee the country. They found themselves, in effect, hostages.

Hostages—the word itself seemed to trigger Jackson into motion. Richard Hatcher, one of Jackson's closest friends and advisers, once looked back at the 1983 freeing of U.S. pilot Robert Goodman, who had been held by Syrians, as one of Jackson's great breakthroughs. "I think that was one of the first times that people in very high places took Jesse Jackson seriously and recognized or realized what he potentially was capable of doing. I think that up to that point that they had not viewed him—they viewed him as basically a preacher, as a person who could engage, who was charismatic and who could engage in rhetoric. But they did not see him as a person who could be a serious player in international affairs and foreign relations."[1]

Hundreds of hostages were now in Iraq. This was a period immediately in the aftermath of the attack, a period when all sides in the conflict had not hardened their policies and were possibly open to suasion. Jackson was not a professional diplomat, had not studied the craft of diplomacy, and had not chosen a career in statecraft. Nevertheless, the man possessed a natural gift for negotiation, a manner and empathy that made those he approached in these crises feel that he understood their position and their needs.

Jackson believed he could bring back the hostages. Soon he was on the phone speaking with Iraqi diplomats. He managed to secure a letter of invitation from the Iraqi embassy. When officials of the Bush administration learned of Jackson's intentions, many were furious, convinced that

Jackson's meddling in diplomatic affairs, his lone efforts at negotiation, would jeopardize their own plans to respond to Hussein.

The United States soon imposed restrictions on citizen contact with Iraq. Now, even with his letter of invitation from the Iraqi, Jackson still lacked the authority to leave the United States to enter Iraq.

He decided to take another approach. For a number of months, Jackson had been planning to launch a national television talk show. Perhaps he could go to Iraq as a journalist! "I *am* a journalist," he told reporters. "Nobody's talking directly to each other...so journalists are filling that gap, the diplomatic gap."[2]

Jackson secured the financial backing of King World Productions, a television producer that ran the *Oprah Winfrey Show* and several game shows. In return for the rights to broadcast Jackson's interview with Saddam Hussein, King would finance the trip.

At the TWA terminal at Kennedy International Airport in New York City, the pilot of the plane that would take Jackson and his associates to Baghdad squirmed through the crowd to shake his hand. "I just hope you get those people out, is all I can say," he told Jackson. As the group waited to board, Jackson, in a kind of prayer, said to those around him, "Now, if the Lord be with us—the Lord be with us—who can be against us? The Lord is our strength, of whom should we be afraid." They were, said Jackson, setting out on the Lord's work.[3]

After long negotiations in Kuwait and Baghdad, Jackson got his interview with Hussein. It lasted more than two hours. At times the Iraqi leader was sullen, expressionless, his movements and speech rigidly controlled. He talked about the injustices rained on Iraq by its enemies. He tried to make the case, a difficult one, that the invasion of Kuwait was defensive, to protect Iraq's ancient rights to oil in the region. He talked about conspiracies to overthrow him and heaped scorn on President Bush, who made no secret of wanting his ouster.

Jackson attempted to persuade Hussein that it was in his and his country's best interest to release the women and children and the sick now being held. "I think you should be secure enough in your real case to make the first move, daring moves that will, in fact, cost you nothing. Say, three or four planes of people coming out of here. Releasing a thousand people, to start with, will cost you nothing. It could, in fact, shift the agenda." Following the long conversation between the two men, Hussein said to Jackson that he felt there was now a "human bridge" between them.[4]

On rising from his chair, Hussein said to Jackson, "It has been a good evening, and we have had a deep human exchange, and in honor of the

Americans who see us on television...you will take the women and children who are allowed to leave, along with four of the men who appear to be sick, on an Iraqi aircraft that will fly you to the United States."[5]

The announcement was startling. Jackson hurried back to his hotel in Baghdad after the meeting and called Lawrence Eagleburger, the deputy secretary of state. There would be more than 200 individuals released, Jackson informed the state department official. They would be dropped off in stops in Paris, London, and finally the United States. As Jackson furiously continued to negotiate, French and British diplomats also worked on behalf of their own citizens.

As Jackson's party prepared to leave on the flight out of Iraq, Jackson had to intercede in one last negotiation. A hotel employee told Jackson that he had seen in a third-floor room an American woman who had been hiding and was seriously ill. When she had heard that Jackson was in the hotel, she left her hiding space and tried to find him. Instead, she was apprehended by Iraqi police and arrested.

For three hours, Jackson fought for this one additional hostage, Faryel Allen of Gainesville, Florida. "She made herself known to me and the authorities became very upset because they didn't know she was under their nose and wanted to keep her an additional two, three days. I thought they were going to punish her," said Jackson. "She fit the qualification to leave. She was an American citizen," Jackson said. When the Iraqi authorities told Jackson that they would send the woman at a later time, he balked. Taking a calculated but enormous risk, he told the Iraqis that he would not leave Baghdad until the woman was included in the passenger list.[6]

Milton Viorst, a journalist who accompanied Jackson to Iraq, said that the reverend's approach "consisted of measured drafts of pleading, rational argument, cajolery, flattery, and moral importuning. But he also made use of our pledge to let the Iraqis know—though there was no menace in the way he told them—that we could not possibly go home without Allen."[7]

The Jackson party did not leave without the woman. The Iraqis finally agreed to allow her to accompany the others on one of the planes out of the country.

By mid-January 1991, President Bush had assembled a coalition of 39 nations and a military force of 670,000 troops and 200 warships. The UN Security Council, meanwhile, had authorized "all necessary means" to remove Iraq from Kuwait if they had not voluntarily withdrawn by January 15. Within in five weeks, U.S. troops, with lightning speed and destructive might, obliterated Iraqi resistance and drove the invaders from Kuwait.

However, for Jackson, the drive toward war—and then the terrible loss of life and massive destruction—was something he would follow on television and in the newspapers, not from Baghdad. He was home now with the hundreds who came with him. Through his intercession and the work of other British and French diplomats, 237 hostages had made it out of Iraq before the war strikes began.

OUT OF THE RING BUT IN THE FIGHT

In June 1992, Bill Clinton, governor of Arkansas, was fighting for his political life in a tough race with several Democratic candidates for his party's nomination for president. As he prepared to speak in Washington, D.C., before a convention of Jackson's National Rainbow Coalition, a relatively obscure rap artist named Sister Souljah, a person whom Jackson had praised for her outspoken efforts to promote black rights and solidarity, had recently raised the ire of many Americans. She had made an ill-advised statement to a *Washington Post* reporter while promoting her album "360 Degrees of Power." In referring to the many race riots that had plagued cities across the country, including Los Angeles, she had said, "If black people kill black people every day, why not have a week and kill white people."[8]

Later, the singer claimed that she was not making a serious suggestion but only making a point and that her remarks were totally misrepresented by the press. She was not literally advocating the murder of white people by blacks, she said. She claimed that she was trying to explain the mindset of black youths whose lives in the ghetto, surrounded by everyday violence, have left them numb to the meaning of murder. Nevertheless, the statement gave Clinton a political opportunity that he quickly seized.

Increasingly through his career, Clinton was strongly supported by black Americans and had befriended Jackson. His support for black issues was at once both an asset and a liability. As he enjoyed the support of many members of the black community and reaped benefits at the ballot box from their votes, he also suffered from appearing too liberal, too close to Jackson. He needed more votes from Democratic moderates to take control of the election. He deftly used the Sister Souljah incident to appeal to those voters.

With Jackson sitting close by at the National Rainbow Coalition event, Clinton said that Sister Souljah's remarks were "filled with the kind of hatred that you do not honor today."[9]

Jackson was visibly infuriated. In front of a roomful of Jackson's most ardent supporters, Clinton had scorned an individual who had earned Jackson's praise. It was, Jackson knew, a blatant political move by Clinton, and Jackson felt humiliated.

For Clinton, the ploy worked. The press praised the candidate for his moderation and for his courage to stand up to the excesses of black radicalism. In the coming days, as an array of black politicians attacked Clinton for disrespecting Jackson at his own event, their criticism further highlighted Clinton's independence in taking a principled stand. For Jackson, the incident remained forever riveted in his consciousness as a betrayal. Jackson demanded that Clinton apologize to a performer who "represents the feelings and hopes of a whole generation of people."[10] Clinton declined to take back the basic criticism he had leveled at Sister Souljah but did express regret at any personal hurt toward Jackson.

Fighting back his immediate instinct for political retribution, Jackson, in the aftermath of the dinner, decided not to turn the furor into fratricidal political bloodletting. Looking back later, Jackson said that he had three choices. First, he could have taken his bruised feelings to a corner and sat out the 1992 election. Second, he could have reconsidered his decision not to run as a candidate. Third, he could have taken the long view of supporting the party. He chose the third.

"The first two would have hurt our team," he said. "I would have gotten some gratification, some vengeance, but it was not the mature thing to do. The stakes were too high to allow private pain to outdistance the need for public policy. And so I took the hit, and then I tried to do more that fall to register and mobilize voters than anyone but the candidate himself. That was the right decision for 1992."[11]

As Clinton gained the nomination and then the White House in the 1992 election, Jackson gave a strong effort to increase black voting registration, to rally the voters around Clinton and the Democratic Party, and to ingratiate himself with the party establishment as part of the team. By mid-October, Jackson had visited 27 states. In taking the road he did, Jackson remained an important political voice and kept himself in position to influence the incoming Democratic administration.

Through the 1990s, Jackson remained a central figure for liberal causes. His voice was heard frequently on television and radio, and he traveled the country lecturing at various forums. He also hosted several television shows, including *Both Sides* on the Cable News Network.

CONFRONTING AIDS

During his rousing speech at the 1988 Democratic National Convention, Jackson declared, "Don't surrender, my friends. Those who have

AIDS tonight, you deserve our compassion. Even with AIDS you must not surrender."[12]

During the campaign itself, it was not unusual for Jackson to raise the issue of AIDS (acquired immunodeficiency syndrome), the modern-day plague so terrifying yet so politically awkward. Because of its nature—a sexually transmitted disease—and because of its principal victims—homosexual men and drug users—the disease, for a long time, remained in the background of political discussion and action, even as it ravaged many parts of the world and became increasingly deadly in the United States.

AIDS was first reported in the United States in 1981. It is caused by the human immunodeficiency virus (HIV). By killing or damaging cells of the body's immune system, HIV progressively destroys the body's ability to fight infections and certain cancers.

For Jackson, the sufferers from the disease and those who were most threatened by it were all part of that large world of the disadvantaged and voiceless with which he had sought to identify himself. They were, he said many times, part of the Rainbow Coalition.

When Jackson visited the Coming Home Hospice in San Francisco and shook hands with dying patients in 1988, he earned their admiration and respect. "I think he's a wonder man, if there is such a thing," said Roger Haynes, one of the patients. Jackson talked about "human compassion without any limitation." Hundreds of supporters lined the streets outside the clinic in a cold drizzle waiting for a chance to see Jackson. "We love you, Jesse," called a voice from the rear of the crowd.[13]

Jackson later remembered the belligerent attitudes about the disease early on in the 1980s. "That's when the right wing was preaching about it as a sin. Not a disease but as a sin. Parents were kicking family members out of their homes when they found out they had HIV." He recalls the time when the daughter of a neighbor who had been a playmate with his children told him that she had contracted HIV and was moving quickly toward having full-blown AIDS. About the same time, another child of a close Jackson friend died of AIDS complications. "And so I became acquainted with [AIDS]," Jackson says, "and had to come to grips with it."[14]

Jackson was determined to use his own personal influence and the political force of the Rainbow Coalition to make a difference in the AIDS crisis. Since the entire issue was wrapped in a climate of shame and embarrassment, Jackson realized that he would need to bring the issue out in the open, to treat it as what it was—a serious public health issue. Jackson was especially keen to interject himself and his organization in this battle because of the effects of AIDS in the black community. AIDS was becoming in the 1990s the leading killer of black men between the ages of 25 and 44. In 1993, blacks made up approximately 13 percent of the U.S. population. At the same time, they accounted for 34 percent of all AIDS deaths, and the percentage was rising.

He lamented the inaction of the federal government to treat the problem with the serious purpose and funding that it deserved. "We are a better people than that," Jackson said. "We are a more generous nation than that. If the president explains the stakes, Americans will step up. In the end, that is the responsibility of leaders—to lift people's sights from their daily concerns, to appeal to their better angels, to lead them to face the historic challenges of the day. This is truly unprecedented."[15]

Jackson began his AIDS campaign in a very personal way; he took oral HIV tests publicly not only to dramatize how simple the test was but also to take some of the perceived stigma away from the issue itself. He made impassioned pleas at churches, persuaded ministers to cooperate in the information blitz, and even gathered together more than 100 preachers to take the test publicly. These were small steps, but all were designed to spread the word that direct action house by house, block by block, and community by community could make some serious inroads against this horrific disease that Jackson saw as the modern-day equivalent to the biblical scourge of leprosy. "Detection, prevention, and cure. There is no downside to taking the test. There's no upside to ignorance," Jackson declared at a rally.[16]

Jackson engineered town hall meetings composed of medical professionals, social workers, and educators to encourage communities to spread the awareness. Joining many other groups and activists enlisted in the war against AIDS, Jackson called for additional government initiatives for prevention, treatment, and research. He declared, "We cannot put out this raging fire with a teaspoon of water." His fight in this war would continue.[17]

NOTES

1. Frontline, "Interview with Richard Hatcher," http://www.pbs.org/wgbh/pages/frontline/jesse/interviews/hatcher.html.

2. Jodi Kantor, "How Does Jesse Jackson Do It?" *Slate*, May 5, 1999, http://slate.msn.com/id/1002773.

3. Marshall Frady, *Jesse: The Life and Pilgrimage of Jesse Jackson* (New York: Random House, 1996), 511.

4. Frady, *Jesse Jackson*, 517.

5. Milton Viorst, "Report from Baghdad," *The New Yorker*, September 24, 1990, 94.

6. Clint Wilson , "Jesse Brings Hostages Home," *Chicago Defender*, September 4, 1990, http://www.blackpressusa.com/history/archive_essay.asp?NewsID= 1190&Week=36.

7. Viorst, "Report from Baghdad."

8. R. W. Apple, "Jackson Sees 'Character Flaw' in Clinton's Remarks on Racism," *New York Times*, June 19, 1992.

9. Jack E. White, "Sister Souljah: Capitalist Tool," *Time*, June 29, 1992.

10. White, "Sister Souljah."

11. "Reverend Jesse Jackson, President, Rainbow/PUSH Coalition, Take Back America Conference Campaign for America's Future/Institute for America's Future," June 6, 2003, Washington, D.C., http://www.ourfuture.org/document.cfm?documentID=1044.

12. "Jesse Jackson: 1988 Democratic National Convention Address," http://www.americanrhetoric.com/speeches/jessejackson1988dnc.htm.

13. Joe Davidson, "For Jackson, the Challenge Now Is to Transform a Campaign into a Lasting Political Movement," *Wall Street Journal*, June 20, 1988.

14. Todd Savage, "Jesse's Campaign 'We Have the Power,'" http://www.aidsinfonyc.org/hivplus/issue11/features/jackson.html.

15. "Jackson on Aids," http://www.workingforchange.com/article.cfm?ItemID =1386.

16. Savage, "Jesse's Campaign 'We Have the Power.'"

17. Brigitte Greenberg, "Jesse Jackson Encourages AIDS Tests," Associated Press, February 24, 2000, http://www.aegis.com/news/ap/2000/AP000211.html.

Chapter 11

THE BUSINESS HUSTLE

It is Saturday morning at Jesse Jackson's headquarters in Chicago, and he is back. At 10 o'clock, he walks out onto the stage, and the cheers of 300 rattle the stained-glass windows of the auditorium, shaking slightly its Corinthian columns. "Life has its dimensions in the mysterious," he says, "You need faith! If you don't know what tomorrow holds, you need to know who holds tomorrow! Don't turn on each other, turn to each other!" Backing away briefly from the podium, he wipes his forehead, looks into the eyes of the audience, and shouts, "Believe!"[1]

In December 1995, Jackson returned to live in Chicago and to resume the active leadership of his organization, now called the Rainbow/PUSH Coalition. Jackson made the decision shortly after his son, Jesse Jackson Jr., was elected to the U.S. House of Representatives. Jesse Jr., who had worked as vice president of Operation PUSH from 1991 to 1995, won a special election to replace Congressman Mel Reynolds of the Second District of Illinois, who had resigned following a scandal. Thus, as Jesse Jackson's term as "shadow senator" of Washington, D.C., ended, the political career of his son was just beginning in Washington.

As Jackson resumed his career in Chicago, he soon began another journey in his own political odyssey. He would take the Rainbow Coalition in a different direction, leading it to fight in a new arena. He called the new venture "The Wall Street Project."

THE WALL STREET PROJECT

The aims of the project were simple and the methods familiar. Using threats of boycotts and the power of Jackson's own brand of persuasion politics (his enemies called it "extortion"), Rainbow/PUSH would lobby companies to name more minorities to corporate boards. It would attempt to persuade or force industries and banks and other large corporations to channel more business to minority-run companies. It would also launch initiatives to involve greater numbers of minority individuals in the country's financial power structure. Instead of fighting outside the capitalist structure, blacks would become full partners in it.

In some ways it seemed to be an odd turn in the road for the civil rights warrior, the leader who had stood for the voiceless and needy. Jesse Jackson and Wall Street—the incongruity leaped out to the casual observer. However, Jackson himself saw the Wall Street Project as the logical extension of the long fight against discrimination, the culmination of the work he had taken on since those early days when he had begun a sit-down strike in the local library of Greenville, South Carolina.

Jackson saw the fight to relieve the plight of blacks in America in historical stages. The first was the struggle to abolish slavery, accomplished through the victory by the North over the South in the Civil War. The second was the fight to end legalized segregation in public accommodations, the fight in which he had participated as a young man. The third was the battle to obtain full voting rights, a struggle in which he had played a role in his political campaigns. Jackson saw the next logical step as breaking down the barriers that separated the minority community from economic independence and power.

Jackson considered the Wall Street Project an extension of Martin Luther King Jr.'s push for equal protection under the law and equal opportunity. The whole thrust of Operation Breadbasket, Jackson pointed out, was that the black community must not buy where they could not work. It demanded, for example, that banks patronized by minorities must be willing to make loans available for black-owned businesses. It also demanded that companies whose services or products were purchased by minorities must be willing to use minority lawyers, minority vendors, and minority construction workers in their everyday operations. That was King's program under Operation Breadbasket, Jackson explained.

The Wall Street Project merely took King's methods to their logical conclusion. "If you look back at the 1963 marching pictures, you will not see one that says anything about dream. It was about jobs and justice and equal opportunity. When we include the under-utilized, we grow; when we developed the undeveloped, we grow. Whenever we include and walls come down and bridges are built, we tend to grow."[2]

It costs money to provide for a children's education, Jackson said. It costs money to have a house, health insurance, and to travel. "Dr. King would say we can be materialistic minded without being mindlessly materialistic. God did not send the children of Israel into the desert without supplies. There's nothing holy and righteous about being without resources to survive. I fail to understand why we should have any reluctance to have a resource base as one of the fruits of our freedom struggle."[3]

In arguing that blacks had for too long been denied access to capital, Jackson pointed to Percy Sutton, one of New York's most prominent businessmen, who in the early 1970s was turned down for a loan by more than 60 banks "We're really in a period of economic apartheid," Jackson said. As he started the Wall Street Project, he promised, "We're creating a new climate. We're telling [Wall Street] you do not benefit by locking people out. You benefit through inclusion."[4]

An experience with the Texaco Corporation in 1996 was a pivotal moment for Jackson in his evolving strategies for pushing equal rights. When a number of Texaco employees made racist comments that were captured on a tape recording, the company faced a major class-action lawsuit. Jackson also suggested that Rainbow/PUSH organize a picket protest. During his discussions with friends and advisers, Harold Doley Jr., a black investment banker and expert in oil and gas, suggested to Jackson that he could be more effective in this corporate setting to attack in the boardroom and not on the street. Jackson immediately went to work mobilizing insider approaches from individuals with contacts with the board members of Texaco. The result was an out-of-court settlement. Texaco publicly apologized for the incident and paid more than $100 million for pay increases for black employees, "diversity training," and other payments. Jackson later looked back at the incident as a lesson. Blacks needed greater economic leverage and power to produce change.

Jackson's Wall Street Project soon had an appropriate address for its office—40 Wall Street, in the heart of the world's financial markets. In January 1998, the master of publicity pulled off a memorable inaugural, convening in New York a three-day conference bringing together a glittering array of financial and political luminaries. President Clinton was there; so was Federal Reserve Chairman Alan Greenspan, Secretary of the Treasury Robert Rubin, New York Stock Exchange Chairman Richard Grasso, and businessman/tycoon Donald Trump. The lavish affair was held on the floor of the New York Stock Exchange on Martin Luther King

Jr.'s birthday. Clinton declared, "If it's a good argument for America to sell more and invest more around the world, it's a good argument for America to sell more and invest more down the street."[5]

Building on the momentum sparked by the launching of the Wall Street Project and a flood of press stories in the succeeding months, Jackson held a "Trillion Dollar Roundtable" in July. This event, focusing on ways to increase investment in needy inner-city and poverty-wracked rural communities and on sparking greater numbers of minority- and women-owned businesses, summoned, once again, the premier names in American entrepreneurship, from Jack Smith, president and chief executive officer of General Motors Corporation, to Franklin Raines, chief executive officer of Fannie Mae. Vice President Al Gore also offered his own thoughts on building mutual minority and corporate growth. Later in July, Jackson also took over the floor of the Chicago Stock Exchange for a gala event featuring Chicago-area business leaders.

All this hoopla and festive partying not only demonstrated the efficacy of Jackson's initiative but also showed that he had not lost any of his promotional bravura, savvy, and uncanny facility for skating on whatever kind of ice appeared in front of him. If government largesse for affirmative action and social programs was vanishing under right-wing conservative administrations in Washington, then Jackson would tap into the self-help mantra of the day. He would find ways to show business America that he and his organization could ride any wave, play on any field, and take on the best competition available.

In looking at the perilous situation faced by minorities in regard to investment and access to capital, Jackson often used the term "redlined," meaning that in the larger scheme of things those who had been redlined had been crossed out. "Look, urban America has been redlined," he said. "Government has not offered tax incentives for investment, as it has in a dozen foreign markets. Banks have redlined it. Industries have moved out, they've redlined it. Clearly, to break up the redlining process, there must be incentives to green-line with hedges against risk." When you place car dealerships, drugstores, and theaters in these areas, he said, the result is an increased tax base that enhances the general quality of life, especially the improvement of the public schools. "My pitch to corporate America is: 'You either are going to green-line redlined America and grow and profit. Or you're going to pay not to grow. What do you choose?' They will choose to grow."[6]

Jackson noted that in the civil rights movement, the protestors and their leaders had been so preoccupied with achieving the basic rights of freedom and equality that they had not focused on the eventual relationship of how minorities must be treated economically. Under the Wall Street Project, they would now focus intently. They would go to where the jobs were controlled, where the money was, and where the opportunities for advancement existed. They would attempt to enter America's capitalist system on an equal footing. "African-Americans," Jackson pointed out, "represent 12.7 percent of the population of the United States. Nevertheless, twelve black-managed mutual funds, comprising almost all of the black-managed assets, represent only $5.5 billion, a very small proportion of all mutual funds."

With the support of major corporations and celebrities and through an aggressive lobbying campaign, the Wall Street Project began to achieve successes. Companies like Merrill Lynch, Prudential Insurance, and the New York Stock Exchange bought into the program, accepting Jackson's basic assertion that the financial services industry had not opened their doors to minorities and must now reach out. "Don't shackle us," Jackson said, "and deny us the right to participate in the global marketplace." Securities and Exchange Commission Chairman Arthur Levitt Jr. announced that his agency would sponsor a number of "diversity roundtables" across the country. "The truth is," Levitt declared, "Wall Street serves America—but it does not yet look like America."[7]

Echoing the sentiments of both Jackson and Levitt, President Clinton declared, "As leaders...as the men and women who have helped transform America into the world's economic superpower, you must help build the bridge between those who work in our gleaming office towers and those who live in their shadows."[8]

Other corporations bent to the wind of Jackson's persuasive tactics—Coors, 7-Eleven, Viacom, Shoney's, and others. Toyota was targeted after running an advertisement that was later attacked as being racially insensitive. After apologizing, the company announced an $8 billion commitment to increase minority management opportunities and dealership franchises.

In some cases, the corporations merely provided funds to advance the work of the project; in other cases, they began to probe more deeply into the problem. For example, the project teamed up with America Online to produce a venture capital fair in conjunction with the Hispanic Chamber of Commerce. The project even joined with the Security Industry Association to distribute to public schools across the country the "Stock Market Game," a board game that teaches kids about investing.

Jackson continued to hammer away about the need for minorities to break into the economic mainstream of American life. On television, in articles and speeches, and at symposiums and conferences, he pressed hard on economic themes. Along with his son, Congressman Jesse Jackson Jr., he published a book titled *It's about the Money!: How You Can Get Out of Debt, Build Wealth, and Achieve Your Financial Dreams!* The book was a guide for financial independence and security, steps that minorities should take to achieve economic self-sufficiency. This was far from sit-down strikes and protest marches, but it was no less vital, Jackson believed, for those in the National Rainbow Coalition to find success.

Federal Reserve Chairman Alan Greenspan, one of the world's foremost experts of world economic matters, essentially agreed that the inner-city, minority market that Jackson hoped to energize remained relatively untapped. "Although the image of free market capitalism has been elevated throughout the world from its sorry state at the end of World War II, the application of it within the United States, its largest adherent, is regrettably incomplete. Too many barriers still prevent the free flow of capital and people to their most productive employment."[9]

As Jackson continued with some success to cajole, threaten, and advertise for greater inclusion for minorities in American business enterprise, the question remained whether corporations responded because of the possibility of benefiting from a potentially lucrative source of profits or whether most companies were simply reacting to the fear of Jackson denouncing them or even threatening to boycott them for not joining in. Whatever the dynamics (probably a combination of both of those factors), many responded to Jackson's push. "Wall Street has walled itself off from a growing emerging market," he kept telling them. "The idea of the wall around China was to be a fortress to protect it. In fact, it locked it out of world growth. In many ways, Wall Street has missed, beneath its nose, a $600 billion emerging market."[10]

The Wall Street Project earned the support of Kweisi Mfume, head of the NAACP. "We have to start thinking about economic coalitions within our own community—not just racial coalitions," he said. "As long as it's separate and apart we'll have a few millionaires. But together we'll have much more economic power."[11]

At a conference for black investors, Jackson said that it was critical that blacks be knowledgeable participants in the stock market. "Imagine a fish trying to live in a world without water—that's what it's like to live under a system like capitalism without capital. You're just living off the 'ism,'" said Jackson. "It's like trying to live off gravy without the meat.

And without the meat, gravy is just greasy water," he said with the hint of a smile in his voice. "Can I get an amen?"[12]

As Jackson continued brashly to exert his considerable influence and that of his organization in the corporate world, he never took his eye off world affairs. Once again, this time in Yugoslavia, he saw an opportunity to make a difference.

YUGOSLAVIA, 1999

Slobodan Milosevic was, for much of his life, a banker. It was not until 1983 that he became active in the volatile and ethnically charged political world of Yugoslavia. By 1987, he was an outspoken leader of the Serbian nationalists in their ongoing struggles against the majority Albanian community.

When Milosevic came to power, Yugoslavia was one nation comprising six republics: Slovenia, Croatia, Bosnia Herzegovina, Serbia, Montenegro, and Macedonia. Serbia was further divided into two autonomous regions: Kosovo and Vojvodina. By 1989, Milosevic was firmly in control of the Serbian republic and embarked on a campaign to consolidate his power throughout Yugoslavia. The 8 million Serbs under his direction welcomed a strong figure to restore what they regarded as their rightful position of authority in the region.

One of Milosevic's first provocative and deadly strikes was to declare martial law in Kosovo and to rescind the autonomy enjoyed by Kosovar Albanians. In the name of Serbian nationalism, Milosevic began systematically to rid the area of all non-Serbs. At first, the process included the firing of all non-Serbs from jobs, closing their schools, and denying them state services. Eventually, it led to mass murder under the euphemistic title of "ethnic cleansing." By 1991, other republics of Yugoslavia, inspired by Milosevic's actions, also began clamoring for independence. Yugoslavia was rapidly disintegrating into a nightmarish hell of violence.

In Croatia and in Bosnia, Serb violence also escalated. In a period of three and a half years, Serb forces killed more than 200,000 civilians in Bosnia and forced half the population to leave their homes. Although the United Nations had positioned forces to discourage the spread of violence, the troops were undermanned and retreated against the escalating horror. In August 1995, President Bill Clinton launched a limited bombing campaign against Bosnian Serb positions and arranged for peace negotiations between the warring parties in November 1995 in Dayton, Ohio.

Despite the negotiations, violence worsened in Kosovo. Throughout 1998, Milosevic increased Serbian troop strength in Kosovo in the face of a number of warnings by Clinton. Through the efforts of a coalition of the United States and several European countries, a draft peace agreement was reached in March 1999. In the end, Milosevic refused to sign, and the violence continued. On March 24, the North Atlantic Treaty Organization (NATO) began a bombing campaign against Serb military targets in Serbia, Montenegro, and Kosovo.

It was in this turmoil that the Serbs announced that they had captured three American soldiers. Once again, the news of hostages immediately engaged the adventuresome Jackson. If he had persuaded the likes of Fidel Castro and Saddam Hussein to release Americans, why not Milosevic?

Jackson made the usual rounds of meetings with State Department and White House officials. Once again, he faced critical reaction to his suggestion of going abroad. The Clinton administration told him that he would not be acting on behalf of the United States, that he could offer nothing to Milosevic that the United States was bound to honor, that he faced great danger, and that the United States could not guarantee his safety. Bombs, after all, were falling daily.

Undeterred by the administration, Jackson was able to secure an invitation from the Serbs. On April 28, 1999, his plane landed in Belgrade. Several religious leaders accompanied Jackson, representing Christian, Jewish, and Muslim faiths. On his arrival, Jackson told reporters, "I would rather try and break the cycle of pain and fear, try to gain their release, than to stand back cowardly and not try." Perhaps his efforts, he said, might provide an opening for the sides to "move gracefully and with dignity, towards the bargaining table and away from the battlefield."[13]

On the bus ride from the airport to a hotel in Belgrade, the clerics held hands across their seats. Jackson offered a prayer: "Bond us as brothers and sisters and as instruments of thy peace. We hope you will be the wind beneath our wings."[14]

Jackson engaged in an awkward series of negotiations leading up to a meeting with Milosevic at the Presidential Palace. As Serbian casualties mounted from the air strikes, Jackson raised the ire of many in Milosevic's government as well as in the Serbian community for having the temerity to show up on behalf of three Americans. Belgrade citizens were living through explosions and air raid warnings and water and food shortages. Hundreds of Serbs were dying weekly. Buildings and bridges were shattering under the bombing campaign as Jackson began talking about building bridges of understanding.

But Milosevic undoubtedly saw Jackson's visit as an opportunity to shape public opinion. Jackson later said that he told Milosevic, "You have to see the power of a diplomatic bridge, not a bloody war." Emphasizing the humanitarian aspect of his trip, Jackson stressed to Milosevic that, faced with a determined coalition united against him, he must withdraw his forces and agree to an international peacekeeping force and the repatriation of refugees. In any coming negotiation, his action on behalf of the hostages would be seen by the world community as a gesture of good faith and goodwill and could help his image. It could help break the stalemate.[15]

After lengthy talks with a number of individuals in the meeting room, Jackson and Milosevic walked out of the Presidential Palace and spent about a half an hour in private conversing in the Palace garden. After he returned to his hotel in Belgrade, Jackson received a call from the Yugoslav foreign minister, asking Jackson to come to his private residence. There, Jackson was given a sheet of paper that said, "I'm pleased to tell you that President Milosevic has issued a decree today releasing the three soldiers."[16]

The released soldiers headed to Germany for medical treatment, a reunion with family members, and a meeting with President Clinton, who was in Europe that week. Staff Sergeant Andrew Ramirez, 24, of Los Angeles; Staff Sergeant Christopher Stone, 25, of Smiths Creek, Michigan; and Specialist Steven Gonzales, 21, of Huntsville, Texas, were now free.

It would be many months before the fighting in Yugoslavia ended and before Milosevic finally pulled his troops out of Kosovo. NATO troops entered the country to act as peacekeepers. The devastation had left the country in desperate poverty, with much of its infrastructure destroyed. Eventually, Milosevic not only lost power but also faced a war crimes tribunal, charged with directing a campaign of genocide against his rivals.

In looking back on the experience, Jackson said, "First, I tried. I was willing to fail where most would not risk being embarrassed. Second, I engaged religious leaders in each country, and worked around the clock to explore every avenue of discussion. Third, I made a clear moral appeal, and organized the support of religious and human rights leaders. Fourth, I listened and learned. I treated our adversaries as humans, not as monsters." He had tried, he said, to help break the cycle of violence.[17]

SPECIAL ENVOY TO AFRICA

Jackson was soon active on another international front. On October 10, 1997, he became President Clinton's "Special Envoy for the President and Secretary of State for the Promotion of Democracy in Africa." There had never before been such a position. Clinton's action was recognition of Jackson's status both as a world figure and especially as a man of influence in numerous African countries. In all of Jackson's trips abroad seeking to persuade foreign leaders to release American hostages, he had never traveled officially on behalf of the United States. Now, President Clinton was conferring on the civil rights leader a diplomatic title.

At the swearing-in ceremony, Secretary of State Madeleine Albright praised Jackson's work and his mesmerizing oratory. "I have sat in the audience... listening to this man weave out of mere words a quilt of reason, passion, memory and aspiration that has enabled out spirits to soar while guiding us across racial, ethnic, gender and social lines to a heightened sense of kinship with each other."[18]

Over the life of his career, Jackson had developed an intense interest in his own African American roots, African culture, and the well-being of the various African nations. His aggressive activity in the war against AIDS was a reflection of the close emotional ties he had forged and the friendships with African leaders he had made over the years. He was especially keen to understand and make a contribution to the evolving political landscapes in Africa, especially in those countries fighting for free democratic institutions and human rights and struggling for economic growth and the end of hunger.

"There are those," Jackson said, "who in a rather contemptuous way say 'Well, Africa isn't ready for democracy yet. You shouldn't impose democracy on them.' Democracy is not an imposition, it's a series of freedoms: freedom of press, freedom of religion, freedom of speech, freedom of assembly, the right to protest for the right without intimidation, checks and balances, separation of powers, independent judiciary. The majority of Africans want those freedoms."[19]

In November 1998, Jackson went on a four-nation tour of West Africa, including stops in Nigeria, Guinea, Sierra Leone, and Ghana. The visits followed a trip by President Clinton to this same region earlier in the year and was designed to reinforce the themes addressed by the president during that visit—that Washington stood ready to help Africa address its security problems, that trade rather than aid should be the focus and goal for future partnerships between the United States and African nations, and that, most of all, the United States encouraged the continuing movement toward democracy in Africa." In Nigeria, Jackson said, "we've not reached the high noon of democracy yet, but there are some very good signs."[20]

In other areas, the signs were not good. Not only had Liberia and Sierra Leone (other West African countries) failed to reach a high noon of democracy, but they had spiraled totally out of control. Both Liberia and Sierra Leone had sunk in a morass of civil war involving a number of cutthroat revolutionists and profiteers who were grasping at the incredible wealth of diamonds, gold, rubber, iron ore, timber, and other natural riches waiting for exploitation.

Throughout the 1990s, warring army units ruled by warlords engaged in despicable torture, mutilation, and even cannibalism, plundering the land and people as they slaughtered each other in battle. More than 200,000 Liberians perished in seven years of war, according the figures issued by the U.S. State Department in 1997. The entire population of Liberia was only 3 million.

Peace agreements were signed and ignored. Cease-fires merely allowed for spent soldiers to catch their breath. Despite UN efforts to oversee elections, intimidation and fraud were rampant. Around any corner could be instant death. On top of all this, heroin trafficking flourished.

The towering figure fueling the crises in Liberia and Sierra Leone was rebel leader Charles Taylor, a flamboyant, Bible-thumping Baptist preacher and gun-running, diamond-stealing ex-con. Erratic, eccentric, a combination of firebrand and showman, Taylor was just as likely to show up dressed in a military uniform, packing weapons, as in an all-white gown, signifying purity and a oneness with God. Before his adventures in Liberia and Sierra Leone were finished, Taylor would face a UN indictment for war crimes against humanity.

Born in 1948 to a family of Americo-Liberians, descendants of the community of freed American slaves who founded Liberia in the 19th century, Taylor studied in the United States, earned an economics degree from Bentley College in Massachusetts, and became a teacher.

Moving back and forth from Liberia and the United States, Taylor took up various political causes, managed to stay alive during a number of military escapades, went to jail for a time and escaped, entered a training program for revolutionary guerrillas run in Libya, and gradually gained a following. By 1989, he had managed to put together a small but terrifying military force made up of various hired guns including young boys and launched an invasion from the Ivory Coast against the Liberian government. The soldiers called Taylor "Pappy." The campaign was brutal, with thousands of civilians slaughtered in a kind of blood sport rampage.

In 1996, the United Nations, United States, and a union of West African states mediated a peace. A year later, in a so-called democratic election marred by fraud and voter intimidation, Taylor won a resounding victory as the new leader of Liberia.

Jackson first met Taylor in 1998. Eager to be seen as a peacemaker in African affairs, Jackson invited Taylor to the United States for a "reconciliation conference" in April 1998. Many Liberians temporarily in the United States and others who had been driven out of the country in the political and military chaos gathered in Chicago at the Rainbow/PUSH headquarters. The meeting gave Taylor an opportunity to present himself as a levelheaded, progressive, Christian leader anxious to bring democracy to western Africa. The conference attendees, including Jackson, said nothing about the murderous trail Taylor had traveled to reach his position of power.

In July 1999, the Clinton administration brokered yet another peace initiative in an effort to quell the violence in both Liberia and Sierra Leone. Nevertheless, the bloodshed intensified. In less than a year, a terror group called the Revolutionary United Front (RUF), headed by a Taylor ally and financed by Taylor himself, had engaged in its own brand of pacification—an assault in Sierra Leone by guerrilla bands who went by such names as "Burn House Unit" and "Cut Hands Commandos." In three weeks in early 1999, some 6,000 men, women, and children had succumbed to the most gruesome ends imaginable. The democracy in Liberia and Sierra Leone had turned into carnage.

In May 2000, RUF fighters even took as hostages peacekeepers sent by the United Nations. President Clinton sent Jackson to mediate. However, in this instance the cozy relationship Jackson had cultivated with Charles Taylor soon blocked any chance that the veteran master in hostage negotiation could again work his magic. First, the government of Sierra Leone, faced with near anarchy, told Jackson that it could not guarantee his safety. Then a group of activists from Sierra Leone announced to Jackson, "Our people will greet your presence in the country with contempt, and we'll encourage them to mount massive demonstrations in protest." Even though Jackson attempted to explain that he was taking no side in the dispute and would be there only to encourage peace and reconciliation, the threatened violence was too much. Jackson's trip was canceled.[21]

Taylor's Liberia was placed under sanctions by the United Nations in 2001 because of its role in the wars in Sierra Leone. Taylor himself was indicted by a UN-backed war crimes court in Sierra Leone on charges that he armed the marauding rebels in exchange for diamonds. When rebels in Liberia organized to oust Taylor and subsequently took over more than half the country, Taylor was granted asylum in Nigeria.

For Jesse Jackson, his activities in West Africa did nothing to enhance his reputation as a diplomatic magician. Indeed, he had fallen under the sway of a hustler. For Jackson's enemies, the whole enterprise seemed deliciously ironic.

TARGET

Throughout his remarkable career, Jackson stirred the passions of both his followers and his adversaries. He was hot button, charged, a flash point for controversy. For some, he was the best example of a self-made man, a gifted leader, a spokesman for the underdog and the underclasses. For others, especially those he challenged, he was a self-promoting, egotistical con man, riding the backs of the press, the public, and his own supporters to a lavish lifestyle and undeserved acclaim.

In conservative circles, taking down Jackson, the arch-liberal, became an obsession, with his every action, appearance, and political stance a cause for ridicule. His economic boycotts were nothing but shakedowns, critics charged, tactics no better than criminal racketeer protection (pay us off, or we will hurt you!). Author and former 1960s radical David Horowitz, for example, slammed Jackson's business maneuvers as "unarmed robbery." "It's basically cry racism and shake the money tree," Horowitz said.[22]

Jackson's foreign adventures, detractors charged, bordered on the treasonous—dealing with communists and dictators without any authority from the U.S. government. His own attacks on industries and individuals on charges of racism, they insisted, were hypocritical, coming from a man who became notorious for calling New York "Hymietown."

In January 2001, Jackson gave his enemies a windfall. After learning that a tabloid magazine was about to release a damaging story about his personal life, Jackson issued a statement admitting to an extramarital affair that resulted in the birth, nearly two years earlier, of a daughter. Jackson acknowledged that he had "assumed responsibility for emotional and financial support since she was born." In his statement, Jackson said that he had discussed the matter with his wife of 38 years and their five children. "My wife, Jackie, and my children have been made aware of the child and it has been an extremely painful, trying and difficult time for them," Jackson said. "I have asked God and each one of them to forgive me and I thank each of them for their grace and understanding throughout this period of tribulation. We have prayed together and through God's grace we have been reconciling."[23]

Conservative commentators took delight in Jackson's transgression. Radio talk show host Rush Limbaugh played the song "Love Child" by Diana Ross and the Supremes as he gloated over Jackson's disclosure.

Even sympathetic observers predicted that Jackson would never again command the moral authority that he once did. "It really damages the Rev. Jackson's credibility as a role model for young people, among other things," said Clarence Page, a columnist for the *Chicago Tribune*. "His biggest problem is with non-blacks, with mainstream America," Page continued. "I think the black community can separate his personal from his public life, but his effectiveness as a mainstream spokesman has been more or less been neutralized."[24]

However, Susan Thistlethwaite, president of the Chicago Theological Seminary, where Jackson received his postgraduate training, said the minister "isn't the first person who has fallen short and won't be the last." As for his moral authority, she said, "If he takes responsibility, makes amends, and doesn't do it again...there is a good chance he could regain [it]."[25]

The incident became such a noteworthy news item that reporters even tracked down some of Jackson's schoolmates from North Carolina A&T to get a sense of their reactions. James Carter, 56, whose older brother was Jackson's roommate at North Carolina A&T, said, "He sought forgiveness, and that is all you can ask.... I don't think in any way this takes away from the outstanding contributions he has made to the advancement and improvement of the quality of life for people in America."[26] Jackson moved ahead to put his personal life back together and keep faith with those who had kept faith in him.

NOTES

1. "Jesse Jackson: The Mother Jones Interview: Populist on Wall Street?" *Mother Jones*, March/April 2000, http://www.motherjones.com/news/qa/2000/03/jackson.html.

2. "Avenue to Diversity," *Newshour*, January 19, 1998, http://www.pbs.org/newshour/bb/business/jan-june98/rainbow_1-19.html.

3. "Jesse Jackson: The Mother Jones Interview."

4. Caroline Brewer, "Jesse Jackson's Wall Street Project Leaves Many Stranded," The Progressive Media Project, http://www.progressive.org/mpbych00.hum.

5. "Avenue to Diversity."

6. "Jesse Jackson: The Mother Jones Interview."

7. Lucas Morel, "Jesse Jackson Finds Wall Street Bullish on Diversity," *Columbus Dispatch*, February 3, 1998.

8. "Clinton Plan Hopes for Billions in Wall Street Investments in Poor Areas," CNN, January 15, 1999, http://www.cnn.com/US/9901/15/clinton.wall.street.02/#2.

9. "Avenue to Diversity."

10. "Avenue to Diversity."

11. Eric L. Smith, "How Jesse Jackson's Focus on the Financial Markets Could Make a Difference," *Black Enterprise*, October 1998, http://articles.findarticles.com/p/articles/mi_m1365/is_n3_v29/ai_21227720.

12. Smith, "How Jesse Jackson's Focus on the Financial Markets Could Make a Difference."

13. "Jesse Jackson Arrives in Belgrade," BBC News, April 29, 1999, http://news.bbc.co.uk/hi/world/europe/331137/stm.

14. *New York Times*, April 30, 1999.

15. Jack E. White, "The Trouble with Jesse," May 10, 1999, http://www.cnn.com/ALLPOLITICS/time/1999/05/10/jackson.html.

16. Howard Chua-Eoan, "Mission Improbable," May 3, 1999, http://www.cnn.com/ALLPOLITICS/time/1999/05/03/jackson.html.

17. Jesse Jackson, "Moral Appeals Too Often Lost in Rush to Battle," *Chicago Sun-Times*, January 6, 2004.

18. Kenneth Timmerman, *Shakedown: Exposing the Real Jesse Jackson* (Washington, D.C.: Regnery Publishing, 2002), 285.

19. "Interview with Rev. Jesse Jackson: Affirmative Action, Wall Street and the IMF," February 23, 1998, http://www.inmotionmagazine.com/jjinter.html.

20. "Jesse Jackson Begins West Africa Mission," BBC News, November 9, 1998, http://news.bbc.co.uk/1/hi/world/africa/210435.stm.

21. Michael Barone, "Dirty Damonds," *U.S. News & World Report*, November 12, 2001, http://www.usnews.com/usnews/opinion/baroneweb/mb_011112.htm.

22. Marc Morano, "PUSH Comes to Shove: Jesse Jackson's Empire Crumbles," CNS News, January 15, 2002, http://www.newsmax.com/archives/articles/2002/1/14/170935.shtml.

23. "Jackson Admits Affair: Civil Rights Leader Acknowledges Fathering a Child Out of Wedlock," http://abcnews.go.com/sections/politics/DailyNews/jackson010118.html.

24. "Jackson Admits Affair."

25. "Jackson Says He Had Child Outside Marriage," *Christian Century*, January 31, 2001, 7.

26. April E. Moorefield and Dale Perry, "Jackson's Hometown Friends Saddened but Supportive," *Greenville News*, January 18, 2001, http://www.greenvillenews.com/news/2001/01/18/200101181310.htm.

Chapter 12

"KEEP HOPE ALIVE"

He will not be slowed.

It is Friday, June 3, 2004. Jesse Jackson is on the road. At Pittsburgh's Market Square, he turns lunch hour into a revival service. With his preacher's staccato cadences injecting beat and rhythm, he calls for outreach to hungry families and jobs for the unemployed. "Red or yellow, black or white, we are all precious in God's sight," he exclaims. "Stop the violence. Feed the children. Save the family. Put America back to work. Keep hope alive. Let me hear you scream." And they do. He invites those in the crowd who have not registered to vote to come up to the stage to get information. The line forms.[1]

It is June 4. Jackson is in Washington, D.C., at the closing luncheon of a "Take Back America" conference. To a group of political and social activists, Jackson charges that the conservative movement is carried on the backs of big money but can be defeated by a campaign with a rich message. A progressive campaign demonstrating a high sense of purpose and mission, he says, can prevail.

It is the morning of June 7. Jackson is in McClellandtown, Pennsylvania, with a group of national and local labor organization leaders who formed a "Reinvest in America" bus tour over the weekend to travel through Appalachian areas of Pennsylvania, West Virginia, and Ohio. Their goal was to fire up grassroots demands for jobs, health care, and better public schools, all jeopardized by policies followed by the administration of President George W. Bush. The problems will not fix themselves, Jackson and other speakers insisted; they must be fixed by political mobilization.

It is the evening of June 7. Jackson is on the campus of West Virginia University—Parkersburg. To an audience chanting "save the workers," he wheels into a spirited attack on President Bush for ignoring the middle and lower classes at the expense of his rich business friends and political contributors. He tells the audience that they must answer with their votes.

Still displaying the extraordinary energy, still moving from one cause to another looking for ways in which he can make a difference, Jackson has lost none of his fighting instincts. He has never taken off the marching shoes.

A year earlier, for example, he stood in London's Hyde Park before an enormous throng of protestors from around the world who had gathered to show their opposition to the Iraq war. Some estimates of the crowd exceeded 1 million people. London's *Sunday Herald* called it the biggest protest ever. "One world, many faces," Jackson chanted. "One message—give peace a chance."[2]

There are few Americans who have generated such admiration along with such animosity as Jackson. Robert McClory, a Chicago newspaperman who followed him for many years, saw Jackson as both "mystifying" and "complex." "I have heard him blessed and more often cursed on an almost daily basis."[3]

President Clinton, in a speech honoring Jackson at the White House in 1999, touched on the principal reason for the visceral feelings brought out in the American public by Jackson's persona and his career. "I think about all those years with the civil rights movement, with Rainbow/PUSH, all the voter education drives, all the long campaigns, always sticking up for issues bigger than himself and for people in difficult situations. Jesse Jackson...has done that most difficult thing in all of human affairs. He has changed the established order of things."[4]

Challenging the system creates bitter enemies as well as admiring supporters, and Jackson was an absorbing figure, blending an almost bizarre mix of passion, intellect, energy, flamboyance, and oratorical skills along with severe abrasions of arrogance and self-promotion and traits of the hustler.

For millions of individuals, however, he meant much to their lives.

James Meeks, pastor of the 10,000-member Salem Baptist Church of Chicago, was 14 years old when he first saw Jackson in Chicago in 1972. Meeks lived in the South Side neighborhood close to the headquarters of

Operation PUSH. From the first time he heard Jackson and his mantras of "I am somebody" and "It's not the bark you wear but the fruit you bear," Meeks became a big fan. "Every photograph of him that I found in *Ebony* or *Jet*, or the newspaper, I cut out and put on a board in my room—I had over 75 pictures." Meeks later became a close friend and lieutenant of Jackson. He accompanied Jackson to Yugoslavia to gain the release of American soldiers. Jackson later named Meeks his heir apparent at Rainbow/PUSH. Meeks said, "Rev. Jackson's influence helped me understand that ministers are leaders who could help people both in and outside the church."[5]

Of all the voices that spoke of the work of Jackson, no individual was more eloquent than 98-year-old Hazel O'Hara of Richmond, California, who, leaning on a cane, showed up at a rally in 1988 to see her "man for the country." "We didn't have no respect," she said. "Just to think where we came from and where we are, it's remarkable."[6]

NOTES

1. *Pittsburgh Post-Gazette*, June 3, 2004.

2. Torcuil Crichton and Matthew Collin, "From Grannies to Jesse Jackson: The Biggest Peace Protest Ever," *Sunday Herald*, February 16, 2003, http://www.google.com/search?hl=en&ie=UTF-8&q=from+grannies+to+jesse+jackson.

3. Robert McClory, "Rev. Jesse Jackson's 'Push' to 'Excel': From Country Preacher to Civil Activist to Moral Leader," *Illinois Issues*, May 11, 1978, http://www.lib.niu.edu/ipo/ii780508.html.

4. Remarks at a "Keep Hope Alive" reception, December 7, 1999, *Weekly Compilation of Presidential Documents*, vol. 35, December 13, 1999, 2534.

5. Edward Gilbreath, "'Still Somebody': Despite an Embarrassing Scandal and Widespread Irritation with His Methods, Jesse Jackson Continues to Be an Influential Voice in the Church. Should Evangelicals Listen?" *Christianity Today*, February 4, 2002, 64.

6. Joe Davidson, "For Jackson, the Challenge Now Is to Transform a Campaign into a Lasting Political Movement," *Wall Street Journal*, June 20, 1988.

SELECTED BIBLIOGRAPHY

BOOKS

Barker, Lucius. *Our Time Has Come: A Delegate's Diary of Jesse Jackson's Presidential Campaign*. Urbana: University of Illinois Press, 1988.

Barker, Lucius, and Ronald W. Walters, eds. *Jesse Jackson's 1984 Presidential Campaign: Challenge and Change in American Politics*. Urbana: University of Illinois Press, 1989.

Branch, Taylor. *Parting the Waters: America in the King Years, 1954–63*. New York: Simon & Schuster, 1988.

Celsi, Teresa Noel. *Jesse Jackson and Political Power*. Brookfield, Conn.: Millbrook Press, 1991.

Clemente, Frank. *Keep Hope Alive: Jesse Jackson's Presidential Campaign*. Boston: South End Press, 1988.

Colton, Elizabeth O. *The Jackson Phenomenon: The Man, the Power, the Message*. New York: Doubleday, 1989.

Dyson, Michael Eric. *I May Not Get There with You: The True Martin Luther King, Jr.* New York: Touchstone, 2000.

Faw, Bob. *Thunder in America: The Improbable Presidential Campaign of Jesse Jackson*. Austin: Texas Monthly Press, 1986.

Frady, Marshall. *Jesse: The Life and Pilgrimage of Jesse Jackson*. New York: Random House, 1996.

Garrow, David. *Bearing the Cross: Martin Luther King, Jr. and the Southern Christian Leadership Conference*. New York: William Morrow, 1986.

House, Ernest R. *Jesse Jackson and the Politics of Charisma: The Rise and Fall of the PUSH/Excel Program*. Boulder, Colo.: Westview Press, 1988.

Hughes, Langston, Milton Meltzer, and C. Eric Lincoln. *A Pictorial History of Black Americans.* 5th rev. ed. New York: Crown Publishers, 1967.

Jackson, Jesse. *Straight from the Heart.* Philadelphia: Fortress Press, 1987.

Jackson, Jesse, with Jesse Jackson Jr. *Legal Lynching: Racism, Injustice, and the Death Penalty.* New York: Marlowe & Co., 1996.

Jordan, Vernon. *Vernon Can Read.* New York: Perseus Books Group, 2001.

Landess, Thomas, and Richard Quinn. *Jesse Jackson and the Politics of Race.* Ottawa, Ill.: Jameson Books, 1985.

Reed, Adolph L. *And The Jesse Jackson Phenomenon: Crisis of Purpose in Afro-American Politics.* New Haven, Conn.: Yale University Press, 1986.

Reynolds, Barbara A. *Jesse Jackson: The Man, the Movement, the Myth.* Chicago: Nelson-Hall, 1975.

Timmerman, Kenneth. *Shakedown: Exposing the Real Jesse Jackson.* Washington, D.C.: Regnery Publishing, 2002.

Wills, Gary. *Under God: Religion and American Politics.* New York: Simon & Schuster, 1990.

Young, Andrew. *An Easy Burden: The Civil Rights Movement and the Transformation of America.* New York: HarperPerennial, 1996.

PERIODICALS

Berman, Paul. "The Other Side of the Rainbow." *The Nation,* April 7, 1984, 407–10.

Brookhiser, Richard. "A Wonderful Town." *National Review,* May 27, 1988, 44–45, 65.

Church, George. "Keeping the Faith: How Two Preachers Are Tugging Their Parties Away from the Center." *Time,* August 18, 1986, 14–16.

Colt, George. "Jesse: A Rare Visit Home with a Sudden Presidential Front-Runner." *Life,* July 1987, 24.

"Day of the Preachers." *Newsweek,* March 7, 1988, 44–46.

Fox, William. "Politics, Not Religion, Trips Up Robertson." *Christian Century,* April 6, 1988, 331–32.

Frady, Marshall. "Profiles: Jesse Jackson, Part 1." *The New Yorker,* February 3, 1992, 36–69.

Gilbreath, Edward. "'Still Somebody': Despite an Embarrassing Scandal and Widespread Irritation with His Methods, Jesse Jackson Continues to Be an Influential Voice in the Church. Should Evangelicals Listen?" *Christianity Today,* February 4, 2002, 64.

Gleckman, Howard. "The Fat Cats Adding to Jackson's Kitty." *BusinessWeek,* April 25, 1988, 75.

Jackson, Jesse. "40 Years Later...Have We Overcome Yet?" *Ebony*, August 2003, 165.

———. "Give the People a Vision." *New York Times Magazine*, April 18, 1976, 13–17.

———. "What Would Dr. King Say?" *Newsweek*, January 24, 1994, 10.

———. "Jackson Says He Had Child Outside Marriage." *Christian Century*, January 31, 2001, 7.

"Jackson's Big Takeoff." *Newsweek*, April 11, 1998, 22–26.

"Jackson: The Fire This Time." *Newsweek*, July 25, 1988, 18.

"Jesse Jackson: One Leader among Many." *Time*, April 6, 1970, 14–16, 27.

Kelly, James. "When PUSH Gives a Shove." *Time*, April 14, 1986, 88.

Kopkind, Andrew. "A Populist Message Hits Home." *The Nation*, July 18–25, 1987, 1, 52–55.

"Marathon Man." *Time*, May 2, 1988, 21–24.

"The Michigan Miracle." *Newsweek*, April 4, 1988, 21–22.

"The Power Broker." *Newsweek*, March 21, 1988, 18–24.

"'Proud to Be Jacksons': Jesse's Kids Steal the Show at the Convention." *Newsweek*, August 1, 1988, 21.

Purnick, Joyce, and Michael Oreskes. "Jesse Jackson Aims for the Mainstream." *New York Times Magazine*, November 29, 1987, 28–36, 58–60.

Serrin, William. "Jesse Jackson: 'I Am...' Audience: 'I Am...' Jesse: 'Somebody' Audience: 'Somebody.'" *New York Times Magazine*, July 9, 1972, 14–20.

"A Split in SCLC." *Newsweek*, December 20, 1971, 27–28.

Thornton, Jeannye, and John S. W. Mashek. "Jesse Jackson Shakes Up Race for White House." *U.S. News & World Report*, December 19, 1983, 35–37.

Wills, Gary. "Jesse Jackson: Newsmaker of the Year." *Christian Century*, January 4–11, 1989, 3–4.

INTERNET SOURCES

"Avenue to Diversity." *Newshour*, January 19, 1998, http://www.pbs.org/news hour/bb/business/jan-june98/rainbow_1-19.html.

Barone, Michael. "Dirty Damonds." *U.S. News & World Report*, November 12, 2001, http://www.usnews.com/usnews/opinion/baroneweb/mb_011112.htm.

Brewer, Caroline. "Jesse Jackson's Wall Street Project Leaves Many Stranded." The Progressive Media Project, http://www.progressive.org/mpbvcb00.htm.

Chase, Robert T. "Class Resurrection: The Poor People's Campaign of 1968 and Resurrection City." George Mason University, http://etext.lib.virginia.edu/journals/EH/EH40/chase40.html.

Foster, Doug. "Jesse Jackson—He Thinks He Can Win." *Mother Jones*, October 1, 1987, http://www.motherjones.com/news/feature/1987/10/foster.html.

Frady, Marshal. "Greensboro Sit-Ins: Launch of a Civil Rights Movement," http://www.greensboro.com/sitins/960621.htm.

"Interview with Rev. Jesse Jackson: Affirmative Action, Wall Street and the IMF," February 23, 1998, http://www.inmotionmagazine.com/jjinter.html.

"Interview with Rev. Jesse Jackson, Civil Rights Leader," http://www.teenink.com/Past/9900/January/Interview.

"It's Time to Give 'Ol Coach His Due," February 10, 2004, http://greenvilleonline.com/news/opinion/2004/02/10/2004021024606.htm.

"Jesse Jackson: A Candid Conversation with the Fiery Heir Apparent to Martin Luther King." *Playboy*, November 1969, http://www.geocities.com/heartland/9766/jackson.htm.

"Jesse Jackson Begins West Africa Mission." BBC News, November 9, 1998, http://news.bbc.co.uk/1/hi/world/africa/210435.stm.

"Jesse Jackson: 1984 Democratic National Convention Address," delivered July 18, 1984, San Francisco, http://www.americanrhetoric.com/speeches/jessejackson1984dnc.htm.

"Jesse Jackson: The Mother Jones Interview: Populist on Wall Street?" *Mother Jones*, March/April 2000, http://www.motherjones.com/news/qa/2000/03/jackson.html.

"The Long Pilgrimage of Jesse Jackson: Interviews with Jackie Jackson, Roger Wilkins, Calvin Morris, Jesse Jackson and Andrew Young." *Frontline*, http://www.pbs.org/wgbh/pages/frontline/jesse/interviews/.html.

McClory, Robert. "Rev. Jesse Jackson's 'Push' to 'Excel': From Country Preacher to Civil Activist to Moral Leader." *Illinois Issues*, May 11, 1978, http://www.lib.niu.edu/ipo/ii780508.html.

Moorefield, April E., and Dale Perry. "Jackson's Hometown Friends Saddened but Supportive." *Greenville News*, January 18, 2001, http://www.greenvillenews.com/news/2001/01/18/20.

Morano, Marc. "PUSH Comes to Shove: Jesse Jackson's Empire Crumbles." CNS News, January 15, 2002, http://www.newsmax.com/archives/articles/2002/1/14/170935.shtml.

Smith, Eric. "How Jesse Jackson's Focus on the Financial Markets Could Make a Difference." *Black Enterprise*, October 1998, http://articles.findarticles.com/p/articles/mi_m1365/is_n3_v29/ai_21227720.

Wilson, Kimberley Jane. "Shakedown: A Shocking Jesse Jackson Biography," http://www.nationalcenter.org/P21NVWilsonJackson602.html.

"You Can Pray If You Want To—A 1977 interview with Jesse Jackson." By Glenn Arnold for *Christianity Today*, reprinted in *Christianity Today*, February 8, 2002, http://www.christianitytoday.com/ct/2002/104/51.0.html.

INDEX

About the Author

ROGER BRUNS is an independent scholar and prolific author of non-fiction and biographies, including on evangelists Billy Sunday and Billy Graham.